BENEDICT LOMBE

Benedict Lombe is an award-winning Congolese British writer based in London.

Her play *Shifters* was originally commissioned by the Bush Theatre, London, and directed by Artistic Director Lynette Linton. Following a critically acclaimed, sold-out run in spring 2024, *Shifters* transferred to the Duke of York's Theatre in London's West End. This marked a groundbreaking moment as Benedict Lombe became the third Black British female playwright to have a play staged in the West End.

Shifters is also in development for a screen adaptation with an Oscar, Emmy and BAFTA-winning production company. Further screen work includes a commission for an original feature film for BBC Films and Expanded Media Productions, alongside other screen adaptations in development.

Other notable work includes her debut play *Lava*, which also premiered at the Bush Theatre to universal acclaim. Benedict was awarded the 2022 Susan Smith Blackburn Prize for *Lava*, becoming one of the first writers in the prize's history to win the award for a debut play. *Lava* also won a Black British Theatre Award and an Off West End Theatre Award for Best Performance Piece.

Other Titles in this Series

Annie Baker
THE ANTIPODES
THE FLICK
INFINITE LIFE
JOHN

Jez Butterworth
THE FERRYMAN
THE HILLS OF CALIFORNIA
JERUSALEM
JEZ BUTTERWORTH PLAYS: ONE
JEZ BUTTERWORTH PLAYS: TWO
MOJO
THE NIGHT HERON
PARLOUR SONG
THE RIVER
THE WINTERLING

Anupama Chandrasekhar
DISCONNECT
THE FATHER AND THE ASSASSIN
FREE OUTGOING
WHEN THE CROWS VISIT

Tearrance Arvelle Chisholm
BR'ER COTTON

Caryl Churchill
BLUE HEART
CHURCHILL PLAYS: THREE
CHURCHILL PLAYS: FOUR
CHURCHILL PLAYS: FIVE
CHURCHILL: SHORTS
CLOUD NINE
DING DONG THE WICKED
A DREAM PLAY *after* Strindberg
DRUNK ENOUGH TO SAY I LOVE YOU?
ESCAPED ALONE
FAR AWAY
GLASS. KILL. BLUEBEARD'S FRIENDS. IMP.
HERE WE GO
HOTEL
ICECREAM
LIGHT SHINING IN BUCKINGHAMSHIRE
LOVE AND INFORMATION
MAD FOREST
A NUMBER
PIGS AND DOGS
SEVEN JEWISH CHILDREN
THE SKRIKER
THIS IS A CHAIR
THYESTES *after* Seneca
TRAPS
WHAT IF IF ONLY

Natasha Gordon
NINE NIGHT

Dave Harris
TAMBO & BONES

Jeremy O. Harris
'DADDY': A MELODRAMA
SLAVE PLAY

Branden Jacobs-Jenkins
APPROPRIATE
THE COMEUPPANCE
GLORIA
AN OCTOROON

Arinzé Kene
GOD'S PROPERTY
GOOD DOG
LITTLE BABY JESUS & ESTATE WALLS
MISTY

Tony Kushner
ANGELS IN AMERICA –
    PARTS ONE AND TWO
CAROLINE, OR CHANGE
HOMEBODY/KABUL
THE VISIT, OR THE OLD LADY COMES TO
    CALL *after* Friedrich Dürrenmatt

Kimber Lee
UNTITLED F*CK M*SS S**GON PLAY

Tracy Letts
AUGUST: OSAGE COUNTY
KILLER JOE

Benedict Lombe
LAVA

Bruce Norris
CLYBOURNE PARK
DOWNSTATE
THE LOW ROAD
THE PAIN AND THE ITCH
PURPLE HEART

Lynn Nottage
CLYDE'S
CRUMBS FROM THE TABLE OF JOY
INTIMATE APPAREL
MLIMA'S TALE
RUINED
SWEAT

Gbolahan Obisesan
THE FISHERMEN *after* Chigozie Obioma
MAD ABOUT THE BOY

Chinonyerem Odimba
AMONGST THE REEDS
BLACK LOVE
PRINCESS & THE HUSTLER
UNKNOWN RIVERS

Suzan-Lori Parks
FATHER COMES HOME FROM THE
    WARS (PARTS 1, 2 & 3)
RED LETTER PLAYS
TOPDOG/UNDERDOG
WHITE NOISE

Winsome Pinnock
LEAVE TAKING
ROCKETS AND BLUE LIGHTS
TAKEN
TITUBA

debbie tucker green
BORN BAD
DEBBIE TUCKER GREEN PLAYS: ONE
DIRTY BUTTERFLY
EAR FOR EYE
HANG
NUT
A PROFOUNDLY AFFECTIONATE,
    PASSIONATE DEVOTION TO
    SOMEONE (– NOUN)
RANDOM
STONING MARY
TRADE & GENERATIONS
TRUTH AND RECONCILIATION

Tyrell Williams
RED PITCH

Danny Lee Wynter
BLACK SUPERHERO

Benedict Lombe

SHIFTERS

NICK HERN BOOKS

London

www.nickhernbooks.co.uk

A Nick Hern Book

Shifters first published in Great Britain as a paperback original in 2024 by Nick Hern Books Limited, The Glasshouse, 49a Goldhawk Road, London W12 8QP

Published in this revised edition in 2024

Shifters copyright © 2024 Benedict Lombe

Benedict Lombe has asserted her right to be identified as the author of this work

Cover photography by Courtney Phillip

Designed and typeset by Nick Hern Books, London
Printed in Great Britain by Mimeo Ltd, Huntingdon, Cambridgeshire PE29 6XX

A CIP catalogue record for this book is available from the British Library

ISBN 978 1 83904 392 5

www.nickhernbooks.co.uk/environmental-policy

Shifters was first performed at the Bush Theatre, London, on 16 February 2024. The production transferred to the Duke of York's Theatre in London's West End on 12 August 2024, produced by Eleanor Lloyd Productions, Chuchu Nwagu Productions, Sonia Friedman Productions, Idris Elba for 22Summers, Maya Jama, Little Simz, Tilted and Tulchin Bartner Productions in association with Kater Gordon and Sayers & Sayers Productions. The cast was as follows:

DES	Heather Agyepong
DRE	Tosin Cole
UNDERSTUDY DES	Charity Bedu-Addo
UNDERSTUDY DRE	Ashley Joseph

Director	Lynette Linton
Set & Costume Designer	Alex Berry
Lighting Designer	Neil Austin
Sound Designer	Tony Gayle
Composer	XANA
Movement and Intimacy Director	Shelley Maxwell
Casting Director	Heather Basten CDG
Costume Supervisor	Laura Rushton
Voice Coach	Joel Trill
Dramaturg	Deirdre O'Halloran
Dramatherapist	Wabriya King
Associate Director	Taiwo Ava Oyebola
Associate Dramaturg	Titilola Dawudu
Production Manager	Chloe Stally-Gibson
Production Consultant	Juli Fraire
Company Stage Manager	Ella May McDermott
Deputy Stage Manager	Crystal Gayle
Assistant Stage Manager	Sarah Back
Head of Wardrobe	Maisie Jackaman
Sound No 1	Andy Hinton
Sound No 2	Iain Audsley

| *Lighting Operator* | Donna Percival |
| *Lighting Operator* | Stephen Thompson |

Bush Theatre in the West End Season Supporter: Charles Holloway OBE

Shifters was originally commissioned by Bush Theatre, supported by Jerwood Foundation.

Special Thanks

Lynette Linton

Daniel Bailey

Deirdre O'Halloran

Paddy Gervers

Tosin Cole

Heather Agyepong

And our wonderful creative team

Thank you for dreaming the dream with me.

Bx

'Love takes off the masks that we fear we cannot live without
and know we cannot live within.'

James Baldwin

Characters

DRE(AM), *a Black man, sixteen to thirty-two years old*

DES(TINY), *a Black woman, sixteen to thirty-two years old*

Notes on Text

Scenes in the present unfold over a number of hours.

Scenes in the past unfold over a number of years.

Dialogue without upper case letters, full stops or other punctuation is continuous.

An asterisk (*) before a line indicates simultaneous speech.

Three asterisks (***) indicates a shift in time or perspective within a scene.

Notes on Production

Scenes are separated in the text but are intended to blend in and out of each other – like a memory, continuously transforming, eroding, shifting.

There is no interval.

This text went to press before the end of rehearsals and so may differ slightly from the play as performed.

I. ALLIES

One

Present. A funeral reception in a community hall.

DRE   (*To us*.) I'm thirty-two. I'm at my nana's
wake.
It's Sunday early evening
and things are coming to a natural end.
I know this – not because the aunties and
uncles
from this community that held her in their
love
are now saying their goodbyes, *oh no* –
best believe that was hours ago
and they are all, very much – (*Quickly
checks*.) yup, still here.

I know this from a quick glance at the buffet
table:
egusi soup, plantain, puff-puff, beef suya,
mountains of barbecue chicken –
now all disappearing at a rate you might
call… 'alarming'
if you were a casual observer.

But to those of us who are seasoned pros –
those of us who've borne witness throughout
our lives
those of us who *know* what it takes to compete
in the action-packed
gravity-defying extreme sport known only as
Grabbing Leftovers After a Melanated Event –
this, right here? That's *what's up*.
No do-overs. No take-backs.
Just win, lose or *die*.

I look up, just in time to see the disappointed frozen smile
on the face of a guest who just figured this out, and I think:
Too slow. The game is the game, sucka.

And maybe – if I was thinking deeply
about my careful lack of deep thoughts at my nana's funeral
I might wonder why I'm pretending my focus is on the buffet
but my eyes keep glancing at the door
and my heart keeps racing.

DES, *thirty-two, enters, slightly out of breath.*

Until *this* moment.

They stare at each other. Carefully, tentatively take each other in. Then finally, DES *smiles.*

DES   Hi.

Beat.

DRE   Hi.

They stand – still in time – as the space itself begins to shift.

(*To us.*) This might be one of those moments when I finally deep what Einstein meant
by 'time is an illusion'.
Because the walls of the world we built
the walls where time is linear and finite –

are starting to crumble.

The distinct sounds of a different environment start to creep in.

And in this moment, I – *you* – are both here and there
and time is moving and standing still
as memory is made skin –

The sounds get louder and louder.

Yesterday, today, tomorrow –
all real, all happening, all at the same time.

And suddenly –

Snap.

Two

Past. A classroom.

DRE   (*To us*.) You're sixteen. You're in Year 12.
               It's your first week, at a new school, in a new
               town
               and you are the living embodiment of:
               'I got in one little fight
               and my mom got scared
               and said you're moving…'
               with your grandma…
               to some place near Crewe.

               South London it was not.

               You're in Philosophy, period three.
               It's a practical lesson on the art of debate run
               by Mr Harris –
               a man who ran debate club in a bygone era
               and now found himself questioning all his life
               choices.

               So my man's out here splitting the class into
               factions
               to fight to the death like it's some *Hunger
               Games* ting –
               only the invitation to volunteer as tribute
               is being met with nothing but sweet, sweet
               silence.

               And then a voice cuts through –

DES   But I don't think I can argue this point, sir.

DRE   (*Mildly intrigued.*) And the voice has an accent –
vaguely familiar, but you can't place it
in this place
where it feels
so out of place.

You clock Harris, now looking both vexed and relieved as he asks:

(*A Northern accent.*) 'Meaning?'

DES   I don't think it makes sense.

DRE   You're getting the impression the voice might do this a lot
coz my guy's already sounding *tired*, as he responds:

'It's just an exercise, Destiny.
Argue for the other side, if you want.'

DES   But I don't 'want'. To choose a side.
Coz there are more than two sides and more than two choices.

DRE   (*To her.*) Still gotta be *for* something
to know what you're *against* though, innit?

DES *now turns in her chair to look at him.*

(*To us.*) And now she's looking at you
and the voice belongs to a face
with –
eyes –
eyes so sharp they could slice through your soul
eyes that seem both too old *and* too young...?
And somewhere in all of this
you notice she might be the first person
in this whole school
who looks like you.

So you say something memorable
and deeply profound:

Beat.

(To her.) D'you get me?

DES   I don't think that's true.

DRE   *(Pressing.)* You don't?

*She turns back – surprised he's still engaging
with her.*

DES   No.

DRE   Why not?

DES   It leaves people out.

DRE   In what way?

DES *is now assessing him with more interest.*

(To us.) You glimpse Harris in the
background, eyes lighting up
as more heads now turn, more ears now prick
up –

DES   If we say there are only two choices, what
about all the rest?
All the other ways of doing things?

DRE   Dunno – maybe decisions wouldn't get made
if there were too many choices?

DES   Maybe decisions shouldn't be the most
important thing?

DRE   How would anything get done if there were no
decisions?

She gives him a curious look.

DES   You're asking the wrong question.

DES *now turns back around.*

DRE   (*To us*.) 'You're asking the wrong question.'

Then she just… turns around
…like she's that guy from *The Matrix*?

Opening chords of Alice Smith's cover of 'I Put a Spell on You' plays.

So this was it, then.
Starting as you would mean to go on.

Two little Black kids
destined to oppose each other
push each other
shift each other

until they could be formed again.

Three

They stare at each other. Carefully, tentatively take each other in. Then finally, DES *smiles.*

DES   Hi.

Beat.

DRE   Hi.

***

Present. Community hall.

DES   (*To us*.) I'm thirty-two.
I have two puff-puff stuffed in my mouth and
– many, many thoughts.
Like: maybe it's *not* possible to inhale two
deep-fried doughnuts with grace.
So. You know. Next time? Don't?
Also: when exactly did my brain decide –
without my consent –

to start calling them *'puff-puff'* instead of
'beignets'
and betray my entire Congolese culture?
And then on top of that:
who gave these fluffy sweet balls of dough the
audacity –
to make my whole heart stop?

Because that's what's happening right now.
Biting into them feels like biting into a dream.
A dream I haven't had for a long time.
A dream I stopped having –
when I decided I don't believe in destiny.

And the irony of it being my name? Yeah, not
lost on me, trust me.

DRE   So you found the –

DES   (*Still chewing.*) Puff-puff, yes. I did. Nana's
old recipe?

DRE   Still remember?

DES   Course.

DRE   I'm impressed. How long's it been, now?
Eight years? Something like that?

DES   Eight years, man.

DRE   Mad.

DES   Maaad.

        Beat.

DRE   And you're in town for how long?

DES   (*Checks her watch.*) Uhhh, three hours, give
or take?

DRE   *Yo.*

DES   My flight's at midnight.

        *He looks at her. His next words should feel
        like they carry everything:*

DRE	…Well, damn.
DES	I'm on deadline, sorry.
DRE	But you're here. Thank you, Des. For coming.
DES	Wouldn't miss it… if I could help it.
DRE	*Did* miss one sick funeral dance-off
DES	don't tell me that
DRE	bet there's a clip making rounds on WhatsApp already…
	(*Falters, less at ease.*) probably with… like… chain mail.
DES	They *stay* chain mailing.
DRE	I'm telling you.
	Laughs awkwardly. Neither can quite believe this is the dry conversation they're having.
	(*Too casually.*) What you sayin' then. You coming?
DES	Coming?
DRE	Was about to get some air and a strong drink. You've got, what? Three hours and counting down, right?
DES	Oh. Well, don't you need to… (*Gestures to everyone else.*)
DRE	Everyone's leaving.
DES	Right.
DRE	You're mad late, you know?
DES	I know, I feel terrible! I was meant to be getting in this morning and then there was this – sorry, no, *very* boring story you – probably don't wanna hear. Could I help now? Maybe? With anything?

DRE	Nah.
DES	Great. Now I feel useless *and* terrible.
DRE	You're not useless.
DES	Just... (*Self-consciously.*) terrible?
DRE	Undecided. Might need whiskey to help me think.
DES	Whiskey, yes. Famous for thinking.
	Both smile.
DRE	That's what I'm saying.
DES	(*To us.*) No, I don't believe in destiny. Coz if destiny is the path laid out for you – you still have to walk it. Choose it. But every once in a while there are moments
DRE	Come on.
DES	moments that make you question
DRE	Join me.
DES	if what you *choose* really matters –
DRE	You got time?
DES	when you've chosen it already.
	Snap.

Four

Past. School gates.

DES	(*To us.*) You're in sixth-form. It's after lessons and you're late for your weekly appointment. It's the one where you choose to sit in silence

instead of talk –
choose to do anything else
instead of talk –
and you're surprised at how quickly
'instead of talking'
has become the highlight of your week.

When you were given pencils and paints and
paper
and invited to dream – you did. Reluctantly.
Now you spend hours each week
seeing the world through colours and patterns
secretly painting dreams and nightmares
and the things in-between
until it feels like second nature.

Maybe you're used to finding a different
language
in the absence of words
in this town that always felt
like someone else's world.
But then again –

DRE   You got time?

DES   (*To us*.) sometimes words come easily.
Like when there's a boy standing in your
way –
the boy who blazed into town with a foreign
ease
wielding his smile like a weapon
and aiming it at you.

DRE   I just wanna ask

DES   (*To him*.) sorry

DRE   hear me out

DES   I need to be somewhere

DRE   I'll be quick

DES   *move*, man.

	DRE *inches closer, and as she tries to push past him he dives back dramatically.*
DRE	Use your words not your fists, bro!
	And then he smiles. It stops her in her tracks.
DES	(*To us*.) You see colours around him – curious colours – light and dark hues, dancing together bleeding into the space around him. Making it feel warmer – when he's around familiar – when he's around even when –
DRE	(*Snatching one of her sketches*.) Yoooo! You *drew* this, yeah?
DES	(*To us*.) He's looking at your sketch of a mother cradling her baby.
	She self-consciously snatches it back.
	(*To him*.) It's just a sketch.
DRE	And you're throwing it out?
	She shrugs.
	Then... could I have it?
DES	(*With suspicion*.) ...Why?
DRE	Coz it's sick. The way you draw. You're proper good.
	She looks at him. At the sincerity in his eyes. And for a second –
DES	(*To us*.) You've grown used to knowing how things will play out before they play out so people only see what you want them to see from a distance.
DRE	I'm serious –

DES	*This* isn't what you want.
DRE	Yeah, it is –
DES	no it isn't.
DRE	How would you know what *I* want?
DES	You want me to join debate club.
DRE	No.
	Short pause.
	Okay, yes –
DES	Okay, bye.
DRE	Look, you're stubborn
DES	and you're annoying. (*Off his face.*) What? Thought we were sharing random facts?
DRE	Definitely ain't afraid of public speaking
DES	you should try being *more* afraid – just – as an *exercise*
DRE	and you always gotta be right.
DES	I don't *always* – have to be right.
DRE	(*Smiles.*) I rest my case.
DES	You rest nothing.
DRE	See? *That.* That's what we need! We wanna enter the national championship next year –
DES	Wanna know what I want?
DRE	What?
DES	Peace.
DRE	Since when?
	(*As she goes to leave.*) Fine fine, I'll be real with you.

No one else... speaks. In debate club. Okay?
It's just been me and this guy George. And
George is... fine.
George is great. George is a top guy, but my
man is *very* into frogs.

DES   What?

DRE   Yeah. *Frogs*. Those green rubbery weapons of
mass destruction that Jesus dropped all over
Egypt?

DES   (*Under her breath*.) Technically that was God.

DRE   *Frogs*, yo. There's only so much a person
should be able to say about frogs –
but you see, George? George will *always* find
a way.

        Beat.

DES   That's the dumbest thing I've ever heard.

DRE   I'm *telling* you.

DES   You just made that up.

DRE   Swear down.

DES   And who's George?

DRE   May you never know.

        DES *holds back a smile, in spite of herself.*

DES   Didn't think this was your style.

DRE   My style?

DES   You're smart

DRE   (*Smiles*.) what you sayin', you noticed

DES   and lazy

DRE   that's rude, you know.

DES   So why're you really doing this?

DRE	(*Shrugs.*) Livin' up to my full potential, innit.
DES	And?
DRE	(*Shrugs.*) It'll look good on my UCAS form.
DES	And?
DRE	Absolutely no other reason whatsoever.
DES	Huh.
DRE	Debating *matters*, Destiny.
DES	Uh-huh.
DRE	Even Harris thinks we need you. And my man *hates* you. But he's right. You're our only hope! *In his best/worst Princess Leia voice:* 'Help us, Obi-Des-Kenobi.' *He flashes her a brilliant smile.*
DES	(*Smiling brilliantly back.*) …No.
DRE	(*Genuinely shocked.*) Wait, what?
DES	(*Pleasantly.*) No.
DRE	But you *mean* –
DES	(*Peacefully.*) No.
DRE	To be clear –
DES	(*Flatly.*) I'm saying no.
DRE	Why?
DES	I don't want to
DRE	why?
DES	I'm busy
DRE	why?
DES	I need to be somewhere, so (*Does the 'disappear' motion.*)

DRE   We could do a trade! Or something? Yeah?
             You help me, I could help you too – you
             know?
             So, what d'you need? How can I help?

DES   (*To us*.) You try to remember the last time
             someone asked you that question
             before they got tired of asking.

             Looks at him for a long moment.

DRE   …Cool. Your silence is mad creepy, still.

DES   (*Lightly*.) I don't need your help, Dre.

             Walks away.

DRE   (*Reluctantly blurting out*.) Okay *fine*! Winning
             team gets two grand!

DES   (*Immediately turning back*.) Interesting.

DRE   So you'll do it?

DES   (*Carefully looks him up and down, half
             circling*.) Okay

DRE   wait, really? It's a yes?

DES   but you'll have to do something for me.

DRE   (*Smiles smugly*.) Sounds like a *trade*, then?

DES   Sure.

DRE   Aight cool, what d'you need?

DES   Your body.

             Beat.

DRE   …*What?*

             Snap.

Five

Present. Bus station.

DES	Nothing, it's just... so strange being back here, you know?
DRE	Yeah. (*A look.*) Strange having you back.
DES	This town feels so... small.
DRE	(*Too lightly.*) Maybe you're just a big fish now.

He keeps walking as DES *stops abruptly, staring up in shock.*

There's this place just round the block, where we can –

DES	Oh my God!
DRE	What?
DES	Is this... the BUS STATION?
DRE	Uhhhh... yeah?
DES	THE bus station?
DRE	...Where buses come and go.
DES	*Wow!* No, wait – *woooooow!* D'you remember what it looked like when we were at school?
DRE	A deserted war zone?
DES	Yeah! But now – look at those curves. That glass. Those boards with bus timings updating in real time? I mean it's... it's... it's... *sexy*?
DRE	...Should I just leave you two alone then...?

DES	(*Distracted*.) huh?
DRE	You and the bus station. Sounds like you're about to get it on?
	DES *laughs*.
	And I'm not judging – hey if 'functional' is what does it for you…
DES	(*Lightly*.) Well, it *has* been a while.
	DRE *stares at her, interest piqued*.
DRE	Has it?
	She immediately regrets saying it.
DES	Okay. Say it.
DRE	What?
DES	Just say it.
DRE	Say what?
DES	You know what.
	DRE *pauses. It could be a million different unsaid things.*
DRE	Say…?
DES	I look different now.
DRE	Oh.
	Not what he was expecting.
	I mean, you look
DES	fat.
DRE	That's not what I was
DES	gaunt.
DRE	Now that's *really* not what I was
DES	'*Really* not'? Wowww.

DRE	(*Smiles*.) Stop fishing.
DES	What, for more insults?
DRE	Don't act like I don't see you.
DES	Where? In the trenches? Hiding from the shots fired?
DRE	You look beautiful, Des. Always have.
	Beat. They both laugh.
DES	Prince Charming, is that you yeah?
DRE	Why? Are you charmed?
	A laugh. A shift.
DES	I'm really sorry, Dre. About your gran.
DRE	We knew it was coming.
DES	Doesn't make it any easier.
DRE	No. It doesn't.
DES	She was a powerhouse, man.
	DRE *nods, clearly wanting to change the subject.*
	And I'm sorry I was late for the service
DRE	it's calm
DES	no, it's not, it's really not, I *hate* being late –
DRE	I know.
DES	My plane was delayed three times – three! There was a whole thing about a storm and look, I get it – everything's a mess and the world is on fire. Sure. But it was like the universe was just trolling me like 50 Cent, I swear! Then when I finally landed my train was cancelled, and by the time the next one was running someone had *flung* themselves onto the tracks which obviously is – is – is – (*Backtracking.*) is terrible, right, it's *terrible*

and I can't imagine what they were going
through...
But by that point, really and truly, *I* was ready
to just end it all too –

DRE   I'm glad you didn't

DES   nooo, quickly climbed off that edge

DRE   coz two funerals

DES   excessive?

DRE   right

DES   well I thought as much

DRE   I'd have to give another eulogy

DES   no thank you

DRE   and that wouldn't be good

DES   sure. Wait – why? Would it? Not be good?

DRE   (*Casually.*) Coz I'd probably just, you know –
           talk about losing all faith in love, how you
           were the one that got away and how my life
           hasn't been the same since you left.

           DES *just looks at him. Eventually,* DRE
           smiles.

           I'm kidding.

DES   Right.

           Beat.

DRE   *Obviously, I'm kidding.

DES   *Right, no, yeah. Of course.

           They both laugh. It's too loud.

           Listen –

           I know I'm not usually the best at stuff like
           this –
           but I'm just gonna take your lead here, okay?

DRE   …Sorry?

DES   I'm gonna take your lead.

DRE   Can you run that back?

DES   Okay.

DRE   What's happening? Are you malfunctioning?

DES   Good, great stuff.
            So as I was *saying* – I'm happy to follow your
            lead, so – in like, thirty seconds, or whatever,
            we can just go back to *not* talking about how
            you just buried your grandma, and the mess
            that's probably going through your head right
            now. And we can roll back to not talking about
            how much I loved her and how wonderful she
            was and my *God*, Dre, how she *loved* you;
            and not talking about how she's probably
            somewhere up *there*, you know, being an
            absolute menace, and, like – fuck, where the
            hell even is 'up there' anyway, right? Like,
            we just tell ourselves these things and make
            up these stories to make living without the
            people we love a little easier, and sometimes –
            sometimes that's not enough. Is it? So we can
            just go back. To not talking. About any of it. If
            that's what you want, we can do that.

            But I'm gonna try something first, okay?
            Don't, like, spontaneously combust.

            She hugs him. Abruptly. Awkwardly. DRE
            stands still.

            She hangs on, hugging him closer. Eventually,
            he hugs her back.

            And we see two people melting into a hug
            that's been eight years in the making.

DRE   How am I doing?

DES   Still intact.

                   Beat.

DRE   Yeah?

                   Beat.

DES   Yeah.

END OF PART ONE

II. FRIENDS

One

Past. Outside a wedding venue.

DRE   *(To us.)* You're seventeen.
        You see her standing outside a venue,
        eyes closed, head to the sky
        like she's imagining she's somewhere else.
        The sun's shining on one side of her face
        and for a second, she looks like a little girl.

        For some reason, you hang back and watch
        her for a bit.
        Watch as someone passes close by.
        Watch as her shoulders tense and her eyes fly
        open.
        Watch as she transforms, in an instant
        from a little girl
        into a warrior
        preparing for battle.

        (To her.) Yo, what you doing here? Stalking
        me now, yeah?

DES   Yes. I'm stalking you. That's what's
        happening.

DRE   It's no fun when you do that, you know.

DES   My dad knows the bride's family. I'm
        basically a hostage.

DRE   Why are you outside? What – you hate
        weddings now?

DES   Don't say it like that.

DRE   Like what?

DES	I don't... *hate* weddings. Just don't – care for them.
DRE	Why not?
DES	I don't know.
DRE	Come on.
DES	I don't know.
DRE	There's gotta be a reason.
DES	Do you always need an answer?
DRE	Do you always need to long it out?
DES	Maybe it's not that simple.
DRE	Maybe you're overcomplicating it.
DES	Maybe you're asking
DRE	the wrong question, right.

A pause.

What does that even mean, though? For real. Is it just something you say to shut people up?

DES	I don't know, is it working?
DRE	Nope.
DES	Shame.
DRE	Give me *one* reason – out of your many reasons.

DES *is quiet for a while.*

DES	I don't know anyone that's still married coz they're in love and not just – coz they have a duty. To someone. You know?
DRE	You just gotta pick the right person, innit?
DES	*Right*. That simple, is it?

DRE	Yeah. Why not?
	Beat.
DES	Why are you *here*, anyway?
DRE	How come you sound vexed now?
DES	I'm not vexed.
DRE	Have I vexed you?
DES	Not yet.
DRE	(*Smiling.*) Yet.
DES	So?
DRE	Nah, I was just passing by.
DES	You... what?
DRE	Yeah yeah, saw the food. Saw the Black people. And I thought, why not, you know?
	She stares at him. He waits.
	I'm messing. I'm working in the kitchen. Nana hooked me up.
DES	Right.
DRE	Church connections.
DES	Cooking?
DRE	Human dishwasher.
DES	Is it?
DRE	Extra coins. Gotta start somewhere before I level up.
DES	You wanna work in food?
DRE	If it makes me money.
DES	You think a lot about money.

DRE	Some of us have to.
DES	Meaning?
DRE	I live on your block. I've seen your dad's car.
DES	And?
DRE	I'm just saying – Nana's done alright for herself, but, like – our house looks like your house gave birth to it.
DES	Funny.
DRE	Your dad's a doctor, right?
DES	Neurologist.
DRE	Cool. So if I ever have a stroke?
DES	He'll pray for you.
	DRE *laughs*.
DRE	You're actually kinda jokes, you know?
	He looks at her.
DES	Why are you looking at me like that?
DRE	Like what?
DES	Like you're about to steal my inheritance.
DRE	Yeah remind me – (*Points inside.*) which one of them rich uncles is your dad, again?
DES	To be clear, there's *no* inheritance, so you can chill. My dad works for the NHS.
DRE	What, he's not private? Later!
	He makes to leave and DES *laughs*.
DES	You saving up for something?
DRE	A plane ticket.

DES	Lads' holiday?
DRE	If we win the prize money, I wanna visit my mum.
DES	Where is she?
DRE	Lagos.
DES	She moved back?
DRE	Yeah.
DES	Permanently?

DRE *shrugs*.

Is that why you moved in with your nana?

He shrugs again with a smile. Carefully casual.

So then your dad is –

| DRE | (*Loudly.*) Imagine! Coulda been on a beach in Lagos, but instead |
| DES | you're here. |

Beat.

| DRE | Man's here. |

They share a look.

It's not every day you see a Nigerian–Congolese wedding.

DES	Would've loved to be a fly on the wall when they told their families.
DRE	I'm picturing that Capulet versus Montague fight. But like a music battle – Afrobeats versus Congolese rumba.
DES	Yeah. It's too bad Congolese rumba would annihilate it.

	DRE *freezes like he's received the wildest piece of information.*
DRE	Nah, naaah, naaaaaaaaah.
DES	Said what I said.
DRE	I *know* you're trippin'.
DES	That there's no comparison?
DRE	(*To the heavens.*) Forgive her Father, for she knows not what she says.
DES	Papa Wemba, Awilo Longomba –
DRE	So we're just gonna pretend like D'banj and P-Square are –
DES	Irrelevant, yes. Yes, we are.
	DRE *gasps.*
DRE	Don't *make* me bring Fela into this.
DES	*Koffi?*
DRE	Sorry, Nana, is that you?
	DES *gives him a look, then takes out her phone.*
DES	Don't act like you wouldn't have this on repeat.
	We hear 'Karolina' by Awilo Longomba or 'Loi' by Koffi Olomide.
	Wait, it's gonna drop.
	It's one long-ass intro.
	Wait wait, it's coming.
	It eventually does drop. They listen and enjoy before –
DRE	Nah turn that off, man.
	DRE *takes out his own phone.*

So you're telling me – when you're coming
out to meet the congregation
you *won't* be playing this tuuuuune –

*We hear an Afrobeats song from over fifteen
years ago like 'No One Like You' by P-Square.*

DRE *breaks out in dance like his spirit is
answering a divine calling.*

He is as ridiculous as he is magnificent.

And as DES *watches him, we see her being
won over by his antics.*

*She starts to laugh, and before he tries to pull
her into the dance –*

'Malachi!'

DRE *freezes. The music becomes muted.*

(*To us.*) You hear an older woman's voice, a
voice you don't recognise
from inside the venue, saying: 'Malachi'
For a second you wonder if you imagined it,
but the voice continues:

'Is that you? You've gotten so big, I can't
believe it!'

The heartbeat starts ringing in his ears.

No. Control it. Smile. Look up:

(*To her.*) No Auntie, that's my brother.

'Such a sweet boy. How is he?'

(*To her, smiling.*) He's fine, Auntie.

'Say hi to him and your mum for me.'

(*To her.*) Of course, Auntie.

*He gives her a friendly wave. Then he stops
the music.*

DES	You have a brother?
DRE	Yeah.
DES	Younger?
DRE	Older.
DES	Back in London?
DRE	Nah.
DES	With your mum?
DRE	Nah.
DES	Where is he, then?

Beat.

DRE   He died last year. Car accident.

Beat.

DES   I don't – understand? You just said he was
           fine?

DRE   No point making a nice old lady sad, innit?

*She looks at him with empathy. He sees it and
smiles.*

           Yeah. See?

DES   Don't... do that.

DRE   What? (*Smiles again.*)

DES   That.
           You smile when you're happy.
           You smile when you're sad.
           And when you're angry
           and scared and upset
           you just – keep smiling... like –
           like you don't think it's safe... to stop. Or
           something.

           DRE *laughs, in that way people do when they
           don't know what else to do.*

So I'm just saying. That you can stop.
Sometimes.

He holds her gaze. Then the scene begins to transform.

DRE   Shit.

DES   What?

DRE   It's shut.

Snap.

Two

Present. Outside a restaurant.

DES   It's shut?

DRE   Idiot. Forgot my keys.

DES   Your keys?

           DRE *laughs, leaning against the door.*

           Is this you having a breakdown?

DRE   No. (*Laughs again.*)

           It's just – it's mad, innit? All of it.

DES   Yeah.

DRE   And you're... here?

DES   I'm here.

           DRE *is still. Serious.*

DRE   I'm really glad you came, Des.

DES   Me too.

           A loud ping.

DRE	Was actually gonna surprise you.
	DES *takes out her phone*.
DES	Fuck my life.
DRE	…still hate surprises, then?
DES	No – well, yeah, I do. Actually. Very much. But – No, it's this storm – also known as *the bane of my life*. My flight's just been delayed.
	Beat.
DRE	(*A smile*.) Delayed, huh?
DES	Fuck my *life*, man.
	Pause.
	Where is this drink I was promised?
DRE	(*Laughing*.) Forgot how demanding you get when you're stressed.
DES	Stressed? Ha! Who's *stressed*? Not me.
DRE	(*Smiling*.) Nah, definitely not you.
	Well… Nana's house is two streets away.
DES	Is it?
DRE	You don't recognise this area? Any of it?
DES	Maybe I just… blocked it all from my memory.
	Beat.
	Besides, you know I have
DRE	no sense of direction, yes.
DES	(*Sombrely*.) It's my one flaw.
DRE	*One?*
DES	Allow me, man.
	DRE *laughs*.

DRE	You haven't been back to your dad's place in a while though, right?
DES	Not since before he sold it.
DRE	So you came back? Before he sold it?
	Beat.
DES	Yeah. Briefly. Like – five years ago. Or something.
DRE	Right.
	Beat.
	Well. I was *saying* our old block's close by. If you don't mind boxes being in the way – one thing Nana always had was great booze.
DES	Oh I remember.
DRE	Yeah? (*Carefully.*) We could just head there, if you want?
DES	Where all the great booze is? Yes, yes, I want.
DRE	(*Smiles.*) Cool.
DES	Wait, why are we here though? You said something about keys? When you were definitely *not* having a breakdown?
DRE	Yeah.
	DRE *points to the restaurant, suddenly nervous. She shakes her head, what?*
	This is my restaurant.
DES	What d'you mean?
DRE	I mean I own it.
DES	What d'you mean you own it?
DRE	I mean it's mine

DES	what d'you mean it's
DRE	running out of ways to say this differently.
DES	Sorry, I – brain. Processing. *Wow!* Congratulations – is what a normal person would say.
DRE	Thanks. I mean it's small, and there's so much I still wanna do with it, but we're getting there.
DES	So you're gonna. Stay. Around here. Then?
	He looks at her. A question.
	I mean, this is *great*, Dre. Really.
DRE	Yeah, thanks.
DES	Business school came in handy, then?
DRE	Looks like it.
DES	And the cuisine?
DRE	West and Central African fusion.
DES	(*Smiles.*) *Wow*, Dre. You really did it. Just like you said.
DRE	And not *one* egg in sight.
	Snap.

Three

Past. Des's house.

DES	(*To us.*) You're sketching the boy who appeared out of nowhere and became your friend before you could stop him and feeling a strange sensation one might call: deep regret.

DRE	(*Changing his position.*) So when you said you needed my body, yeah
DES	sit *still*
DRE	(*Changing position.*) and wouldn't tell me why
DES	this is not *still*
DRE	(*Changing position.*) I thought you meant like
DES	keep doing what you're doing
DRE	like you were gonna harvest my organs or
DES	but the opposite, where you're *still*?
DRE	use me as a human sacrifice or – something a bit more... exciting. (*Starts yawning partway through.*)
DES	There's still time, don't worry.
DRE	(*Still yawning and stretching.*) Can we take a break?
DES	(*To herself.*) Who would miss him? If I killed him?
DRE	Got any food?
DES	Food?
DRE	Sustenance. For the brain. Heard of it?
DES	(*Looks at him in curious amusement.*) Huh.
DRE	What?
DES	You're hangry
DRE	nah
DES	(*Growing amusement.*) you are, that's what it is, you're *hangry*
DRE	said I'm not though
DES	it's cute

DRE	(*Smoothly.*) then I'm hangry, yeah
DES	in like a Fred Flintone sad-caveman kinda way.
	He looks at her as she enjoys her own joke.
	'Got any food?' 'Yabadaba-doo?'
DRE	(*Unsmiling.*) HAHAHAHA whereisthefooooood?
DES	Check the fridge.
	He mumbles grumpily as he walks to the fridge:
DRE	(*Under his breath.*) talkin' bout 'Yabadaba-doo', he don't even say it like that.
	He looks in the fridge. After a moment, with deep disappointment:
	You have an egg.
DES	What?
DRE	*One* egg.
DES	Okay.
DRE	Nah. Not okay. What d'you lot eat, man?
DES	Dunno, whatever.
DRE	What d'you mean 'whatever'?
DES	Like – whatever.
DRE	Who cooks?
	DES *laughs.*
DES	Oh, you were serious. No one cooks.
DRE	Everyone can cook.
DES	Didn't say we can't. We just don't. In this house.

DRE   Why not?

DES   Used to. When we were in London with my
             mum when she was around. But I was like –
             ten or eleven so.
             I don't remember. How to make her food.
             How to make it... taste right, I guess.

DRE   Whereabouts in London again?

DES   South.

DRE   I knew I liked you! (*Off her look*.) ...bro.

             Pause.

             So you moved here with your dad, after your
             mum

DES   Yeah.

DRE   How did she

DES   Brain tumour.

DRE   Damn. Sorry.

DES   Ironic, no? Marrying a neurologist and still
             dying of a brain tumour.

             Beat.

             It's strange though.
             No one tells you how to do it. When you're a
             kid. It's like –
             One day you have a mum. Next, you don't.
             But no one tells you – how to remember
             that she was yours. And you were hers.
             And you *belonged* – to someone.
             Once. You know?

             No one tells you. Do they?
             Then you start to forget things.
             Like how her food tasted.

             Beat.

DRE	Describe it to me. Your mum's food. How did she make it?
DES	Oh.
DRE	Gimme some inspiration while I cook us this... egg.
DES	Uhhh... Well. She'd start off with music. Always. That's how we knew it was about to pop off in the kitchen.
DRE	Play something, then. Something she'd play.

DES *starts to play 'Yolele' by Papa Wemba.*

	What's this?
DES	Old-school. Papa Wemba.

DRE *listens for a few beats.*

DRE	Kinda slaps.
DES	I told you!

They listen as the lyrics kick in.

DRE	What's he singing about?

DES *listens.*

DES	Someone he lost.

Beat.

DRE	Tell me more about her food.
DES	There's this one dish she'd make a lot. It's called *ngai-ngai.*
DRE	(*Slowly.*) *Ngai-ngai.*
DES	Your Lingala's pretty good.
DRE	Thanks.

DES   So 'ngai' means sour.

DRE   'Sour-sour.'

DES   *Exactly.* And it's like this – like kinda tangy spinach
                but not actually spinach, like – like –
                roselle leaves, I think that's what they're called,
                these roselle leaves that you can cook with eggplant stew
                and onions and chilli flakes and add in fried or steamed fish and –

                She does a chef's kiss.

                Just – the best.

                The song continues playing as if in a different time.

                I remember us all dancing to this.
                And Papa didn't dance.
                But sometimes. For her. He did.

                She watches echoes of them across the room, with the most content, childlike smile.

DRE   And voilà.

                It's not *ngai-ngai*, obviously, man only had an egg –
                but mixed in some bread, some milk, dash of cinnamon –

DES   (*To us.*) The smell is what hits you first.

DRE   What d'you think?

DES   (*To us.*) The sweet cinnamon claws at your throat
                circles around your ribcage like a rope
                obstructing your ability to breathe.

DRE   ...Des?

DES   (*To us.*) It lifts you up and up and out – of
             yourself.
             Smells are funny, right?
             You forget the power they hold
             to make nightmares come alive.

DRE   Des, what's wrong?

DES   (*To herself, breathing out.*) Not now not now
             not now, no, no, no

DRE   (*Reaching out for her.*) Des?

DES   (*Struggling to breathe.*) No, stay – there –
             please!

DRE   I think… I think you're having a panic attack.

DES   No I'm not

DRE   okay

DES   I'm *not*

DRE   okay you're not, just keep breathing

DES   I'm trying

DRE   deep breaths

DES   I'm *trying*!

DRE   Just in and out

DES   Stop talking!

DRE   Sorry

DES   wait keep talking

DRE   you want me to

DES   yes, keep talking!

DRE   Okay, close your eyes.

DES   Don't tell me what to do!

             She immediately closes her eyes.

             Okay they're closed, now what?

DRE	Cross your hands, put 'em on your chest. That's it. Now lock your thumbs together... kind of like a butterfly. Good. Now start tapping your hands on your chest, slowly. *Slowly*, Des. And keep breathing. In and out, that's it. Slowly. In and out.
	He breathes with her – until her breath finally starts to steady.
	Feeling any better?
	She nods. He doesn't ask 'What was that about?' but she feels his question in the silence.
DES	It just – happens. Sometimes.
DRE	When did it start?
DES	I don't... know.
DRE	My brother – Malachi – he used to get them a lot, too.
DES	Your brother?
DRE	Yeah. He had to do that a lot.
	When he points to the placement of her hands on her chest like a butterfly, DES *looks around awkwardly, suddenly realising she's still crouched on the floor.*
	DRE *now kneels, cautiously drawing closer as if approaching a wild animal.*
	I'm gonna try something, yeah?
	(*At her uncertain look.*) Don't, like, spontaneously combust.
	And he hugs her. She stiffens. He continues to hug her.

Eventually, she relaxes into the hug.
We see her start to hug him back – but she
drops her hands at the last minute.
After a moment, DRE *pulls back a little to*
look at her.

DES   (*To us*.) And now he's staring at you
           and you wonder if he sees, if he knows
           if he's reaching into the darkest ugliest corners
           and scooping out the truth.

DRE   I'm never cooking an egg again, I swear
           down.

           DES *smiles. He helps her up. The scene*
           begins to transform.

           Sorry about all the boxes.

           Snap.

Four

Present. Nana's house.

DES   Wow, it's like an obstacle course.

DRE   You were warned.

DES   I – was warned.

DRE   Sorry –

DES   Don't be silly

DRE   I was packing up Nana's things last week

DES   don't worry

DRE   tryin'a work out what to hold on to,
           what to let go.

           He pauses.

           Harder than I thought.

DES   Can I help?

               He looks at her.

DRE   Okay.

               *He makes her a drink as she starts sifting
               through boxes.*

               It's mad weird though. Don't think I ever
               believed in ghosts before –
               but now I'll walk into a room – and there she
               is.
               Playing blues on vinyl. Laughing in the
               kitchen. Cussing me out.

DES   She did that a lot.

DRE   She did.

DES   Cussed me out a few times, too.

DRE   No soul was spared.

DES   Can't say she wasn't fair.

DRE   Started to see you too, you know.

DES   What d'you mean?

DRE   Here. In the house.

DES   Like... a ghost? Or something?

DRE   Or something.

DES   You know, I had this conversation with one of
               my friends the other day.
               We were talking about how memory shapes
               our reality

DRE   right

               He hands her a drink.

DES   thanks –
               and I'm probably oversimplifying it, coz,
               she's a whole neuroscientist and I'm –

in comparison – an idiot, but basically we were discussing how we can never remember things in the same way – because *we* are never the same, right? Even now, when I'm trying to remember the conversation I had with her, my mind's already modified it. Coz we can't help but make meaning out of what we know in the present, right? And the meaning we make of our lives changes how we remember things. So, the act of remembering, I guess, the act itself, of telling a story – changes it? Which is –

DRE   terrifying

DES   *right?*

DRE   Coz then how many stories will actually be true?

DES   Well, that's just it! If we're all reconstructing our own truth, that means there's no single truth, so I guess – I dunno –
I guess then we're kind of just asking: what is... 'truth'?

           Beat.

DRE   So d'you make a habit of bringing innocent men into existential crisis
or am I special?

DES   You're special.

DRE   You're a liar.

DES   (*Laughs.*) So am I still a ghost? 'Or something'?

DRE   A ghost made real.

           Beat. They share a look.

           Said you were on deadline?

DES	Yeah, man.
DRE	Are you still
DES	a female version of a hustla?

DRE smiles.

DRE	Come on now.
DES	Yeah, still on my freelance shit.
DRE	Heard you're kind of a big deal.
DES	Ummmm... *where*?
DRE	Why you lyin'?
DES	I'm not! Who's your source? Oh God, it's not my dad, is it? You know he still doesn't understand what I do? He just keeps telling everyone I'm a 'conflict journalist'

They both laugh.

Seriously! And I don't know if it's just because, like, as a rule
telling your African father that you're a '*concept artist*'
just like... breaks them? Forever? Or something? You know?
Or if he genuinely believes I'm out there in war zones doing important work.
Either way, I'm definitely a disappointment as a Congolese daughter, so.

DRE	Impossible.

She means it to come off lighter than it does:

DES	Oh, it's possible. Trust me.

Pause.

But the work is so varied you know?

Like, right now I'm working on this animated
thing
and before that I was pulling together an
exhibition in Venice
and just like *losing* my mind every day, until –

DES *stops – pulling something out of a box.*
She holds up a book.
Looks at him – amused, confused and touched
all at once.

Wait – *how*? How is *this* – here?
You've... read my illustrated children's
books?

Beat.

DRE	Nana would get them.
DES	*Really?*
DRE	Yeah she kept tabs on you through the years. She was really proud of you, you know?
DES	Thanks, that means a lot.
DRE	Plus – my son's a fan.

DES *takes a beat. Like she knew it was*
coming but it still blindsides her.
And then, carefully, casually:

DES	Your son? *Really?* He likes... dark fairy tales?
DRE	Well, he likes the pictures.
DES	That's sweet. How old is he?
DRE	Turned five this year.

Pause.

DES	*Five.* Wow.
DRE	Yeah. I don't know how that happened.

Beat.

DES	Well, Dre, when a man and a woman *love* each other very much –
	She expects him to laugh, but he doesn't.
	Come on, that was funny
DRE	sorry
DES	*not even a pity laugh?
DRE	*sorry, yeah – ha-ha-ha.
DES	Jesus
DRE	sorry
DES	that was really
DRE	bad, I agree. Rewind?
DES	Yup. (*As if for the first time.*) So you have a son?
DRE	Yeah!
	DES *laughs.*
DES	(*Genuine curiosity.*) What's he like?
DRE	Oh man, he's great.
DES	Yeah?
DRE	Yeah, he's kind and he's curious and he's hella smart too, man. And *I know* how it always is, everyone thinks their kid's a genius for just existing and sharing their DNA, but swear down this kid –
DES	is a genius for just existing and sharing your DNA?
	They both laugh.
DRE	I'll be honest, I struggled at first, you know.
DES	Parenthood didn't come easily? *No way.*

DRE | Look I'm just saying, you know –
you expect it'll be tough and you'll get things wrong
and you'll feel lost or overwhelmed or whatever.

But then when you're struggling to get medical diagnoses,
or worrying about why he's not speaking yet
or why he's not like 'other' kids
or whatever story you've told yourself 'normal' is
– that just opens up so many other things.

DES | Like what?

DRE | Like... my kid didn't start speaking till he turned four, right?
And I look back now and I just feel – guilty.

DES | Why?

DRE | Coz I spent so long thinking we needed to fix him. You know?
Then one day, I was speaking to him – and he does this thing, right
he does this thing where he doesn't really look you square in the eye
so his viewpoint is always a bit... off, like, a bit off-kilter you know?
And he's responding to me, and in that moment –
I *see* him. D'you get me? Like, I finally clock that my son, literally
found a different way of seeing the world. And being in it.
No less 'normal' than any other kid. Just different. You know?
And coz I panicked, coz I got scared, I just forgot. To listen.
He reminded me there are so many different ways of communicating.

And instead of trying to change him –
I just had to meet him where he was. Just had
to pay attention.

DRE *notices* DES *is uncharacteristically
silent.*

Anyway, I know it's not groundbreaking or
anything –
but it changed a lot for me.

DES   That's really beautiful, Dre

DRE *shakes it off.*

no, I mean it.
Just imagine... if we all had *that*. God,
imagine...

Beat.

Good to see I was right, anyway.

DRE   About what?

DES   You.

*She starts looking around as the scene begins
to transform.*

DRE   You alright?

Snap.

Five

Past.

DES   My painting. I can't – find it?

DRE   What d'you mean?

DES   For my portfolio. 'The Fugitives'. How does a
painting just *disappear*?

DRE	You named a painting... 'The Fugitives'? And it's just gone... and escaped?
	DES *laughs*.
	***
	Present. Nana's house.
DES	Wait, you have this on vinyl?
	She holds up a vinyl record of John Hiatt & The Goners's 'Have a Little Faith in Me'.
DRE	Found it in Nana's stuff.
DES	*Whoa.*
	Beat.
	D'you remember when we – ?
	She stops herself, shaking her head. He waits.
DRE	When we what?
DES	Nothing.
	He watches her as she starts to put the record back. Casually takes it from her before she does.
DRE	I remember.
	Beat.
	Wanna play it?
DES	(*Too lightly.*) Sure. If we can find something to play it on.
DRE	Help me look?
DES	Course.
	They start sifting through boxes. DRE *surreptitiously glances at* DES.
	(*Without turning.*) What?

DRE	Hm?
DES	Can feel your eyes on me, you ain't slick.
DRE	Oh.
DES	Spit it out.
DRE	Nah, it was just – I heard that you got engaged recently?
	DES *stops sifting briefly.*
DES	You heard?
DRE	Yeah, well, it was just you know – *word*
DES	huh
DRE	on the street
DES	uh-huh.
	Beat.
DRE	So...?
DES	I did.
DRE	Oh yeah?
DES	Yeah. His name's Travis. He's a good man, you know? Kind, chill. A jazz musician. Tours a lot.
	DRE *puts on a smile.*
DRE	Yeah. Cool. Cool. Cool cool cool cool. I mean, congrats – Des that's – really – great.
	After a silence:
	It's just – I mean, it's kinda funny, ain't it? Coz you always said you'd never
DES	yeah.

DRE	But now you're
DES	(*Firmly.*) yeah.
DRE	So I'm just
DES	(*Turns to look.*) what?
DRE	…curious.
DES	Right.
DRE	What?
DES	Nothing.

She continues sifting.

DRE	And… This guy – Tyler, was it? Timmy? Travis? He's… the one?
DES	(*Too loudly.*) Found it!

DES pulls out a gloriously vintage vinyl record player.

Snap.

Six

Past. Nana's house.

DRE	Oh yeah? Hit me!
DES	Okay. Quick-fire – *For…* the end of the world. Go!
DRE	…Why would I argue for the end of the world?
DES	You should know your opponent's argument.
DRE	But there's no argument.

DES	Prove it.
DRE	Number one: we would all be dead.
DES	Would we?
DRE	Yeah, man.
DES	How do we know that? Have we tried it?
DRE	…Have we tried it?
DES	Sure.
DRE	Have we tried to *end the world*?
DES	Have we?
DRE	So you're a Bond villain now?
DES	How do we know it would be the end of life? Whose version of life?
DRE	Ours. Our lives.
DES	I would argue the world's already ended though.
DRE	So we're in a simulation?
DES	We wish.
DRE	Not me. Me not wish.
DES	What if we were?
DRE	In a simulation?
DES	Wouldn't you wanna see what was beyond all this?
DRE	Aliens? Nah.
DES	Think about it, man!
DRE	I have
DES	Every time the world's ended it's been on someone else's terms. Right? Because *someone* decided some people

deserve to live
and others don't
and the rest of us just live in this-this-this
space in-between.
But what if we could start over?
Or break-free of the simulation?
We *know* this isn't all there is –
and we know this isn't *working*.
So who's to say the answer isn't in starting
over?
Or in trying? Right? *Right?*
Wait for it – maaaybe – the world has to *end*
for life to *survive*?

*She looks at him like she really thinks she just
did something here.*

*He stares back blankly for a long moment,
then smiles as the space begins to shift.*

DRE   That's actually not bad, you know.

             Snap.

Seven

Present. Nana's house.

DES   And by 'not bad' d'you mean the opposite?

DRE   You got jokes now?

DES   I'm just saying, it looks broken.

DRE   It's not broken, it's just, you know

DES   prehistoric?

DRE   Exactly!

DES   (*Laughing.*) That's not good, though!

DRE	Means I can fix it.
DES	You fix old record players now?
DRE	Why not?
	He begins tinkering with it. She watches him, smiling.
DES	You were always saying that when we were growing up.
DRE	What?
DES	'Why not?' Diving into everything and driving me mad.
DRE	Now look at me. Responsible for an actual human life.
DES	Big moves.
DRE	Don't get me started on all the ways I could mess him up.
DES	Oh you're definitely gonna mess him up.
DRE	*Wow.*
DES	Everyone messes up their kids, man!
DRE	'preciate the faith.
DES	The act of being *born* basically messes us up. Our brains just protect us – from remembering. But we're all survivors of... something, right?
DRE	...this is a *pep talk*, yeah?
DES	I was getting there.
DRE	Coz what I'm *hearing* is 'we're all broken and there's no hope'.
DES	I think we can still make something beautiful. Out of broken things. If we're careful.
	He holds her gaze.

DRE   I'll hold you to that, yeah?

                       Then, after a moment:

                       Badabing, badaboom!

                       He points to the record player.

                       Fixed it.

                       *We hear the preliminary hiss, the scratch of
                       the nail on vinyl – and finally, we hear John
                       Hiatt's silky smooth tones as 'Have a Little
                       Faith in Me' begins to play.*

Eight

*Past. Nana's house. 'Have a Little Faith in Me' plays gently in
the background.*

DRE   (*To us.*) You're eighteen. Summer's here.
                       It's the end of your final year of sixth-form
                       and the night of the debating competition.
                       But you're standing outside Nana's front
                       doorstep –
                       hours earlier than expected.
                       You can hear her music streaming from the
                       kitchen window
                       reminding you that it's her Big Night In
                       that you're shortly about to interrupt with –

DES   Dre, I'm sorry

DRE   (*To her.*) don't be

DES   I am, I *should* be, I mean – it's never actually

DRE   Des

DES   happened before, not like that, not in public

DRE	it's okay
DES	it's not *okay*
DRE	I promise you
DES	I should've been
DRE	it's okay
DES	better, smarter
DRE	Des
DES	don't know how this happened
DRE	It's okay
DES	I can do this stuff in my *sleep*
DRE	I know, it's okay
DES	and stop saying that!
DRE	What d'you want me to say?
DES	I don't know!
DRE	Good, helpful.
DES	Say you're pissed off!
DRE	Well I'm not
DES	Say I messed up!
DRE	You didn't
DES	Say I had a panic attack on the *one* day I just needed to keep my shit together after all the time we spent practising – I feel so – *stupid*!
DRE	You're not.
DES	And there goes the two grand!
DRE	Doesn't matter.
DES	And the plane tickets? Your mum?

DRE	I'll figure something else out.
DES	And what if you can't get into uni now? We said we'd both go back to London but maybe –
DRE	Des
DES	You hate me
DRE	nah, man
DES	you do
DRE	I don't
DES	your eyes are doing that thing
DRE	what thing?
DES	that thing they do when they hate people.
DRE	(*Laughing*.) Des!
DES	What? Why are you laughing?
DRE	Because! It stopped being about any of that… for me.
DES	But you said
DRE	I know what I said.
DES	Then what was it about?
	Beat.
DRE	What do you think, Des?
	He stares at her. She stares at him. *'Have a Little Faith in Me' now starts to play more audibly.*
DES	You… are an idiot.
	He shrugs.
DRE	…Yeah.
	DES *softens. Unthinkingly leans forward to swiftly peck him on the cheek.*

Wherever she intended, she actually catches him on the corner of his mouth and DRE *instinctively puckers his mouth, surprised.*

He straightens, staring down at her intently. DES, *equally surprised, stares back at him. And then – shakes her head. Shit. Shit-shit-shit.*

DES *turns to walk away. But* DRE *reaches out for her arm and as she spins around, he lowers his head to kiss her.*

She meets him in a long, hard, passionate kiss
their arms pulling each other close
their hands uncertain
the full length of their bodies leaning into each other.

The music swells.

They break the kiss and for a brief moment continue to hold each other.

END OF PART TWO

III. FRACTURES

One

DES	(*To us*.) The first fairy tale you ever illustrate shows a little Black girl on a cloud looking down at a tiny boy on the ground who has an arm outstretched.

You call it 'The Girl Who Floated Away'.

***

Present. Nana's house. They are a few drinks in. |
DRE	Wait, American?
DES	Yeah, they were launching the books in the States so I was there on, like, the world's tiniest book tour and Travis was on a break from touring with his, you know
DRE	jazz band.
DES	Right.
DRE	Huh.
DES	I didn't need anything from him. He didn't need anything from me.
DRE	Huh.
DES	And it just – worked. You know?
DRE	*Huh*.
DES	What?
DRE	Just sounds… easy.

DES	(*Smiling.*) It was.
DRE	Too easy.
DES	What's wrong with easy?
DRE	No one writes songs about things that come easy.

She gives him a look.

DES	First of all, that's a lie. I can think of a million songs right now.
DRE	A million.
DES	Yes.
DRE	(*Getting his phone out.*) Aight cool. Name... one?
DES	(*Smugly.*) 'Easy' Lionel Richie and the Commodores.
DRE	It's actually pronounced the *Commodorés*.
DES	...no it's not?
DRE	okay it's not, but it should be, no?

They laugh and start to play 'Easy' by the Commodores.

DRE pointedly sings the opening lines of the song. Then turns to smile at a much less smug looking DES.

DES	Forgot... what the song was about.
DRE	Clearly.
DES	My point still stands.
DRE	Where? On the floor?
DES	You know there's loads more though!
DRE	Like?

She thinks.

DES	(*Less certain.*) That DaniLeigh one?
DRE	Now you're just picking random songs called 'Easy'.
DES	I know!
DRE	Last shot at redemption. Final answer?
DES	(*Dramatically.*) Lock it in.

'Easy' by DaniLeigh plays.

As soon as the tune drops, both forget the point they're trying to prove – and just instinctively start vibing to it.

It starts off as both just individually enjoying the song, and then subtly grows into them dancing together, like it's second nature.

It feels familiar and playful and joyous – then, as both increasingly become aware of being in each other's space it starts to shift into something more intimate – and dangerous.

DES *pulls away, laughing and playing it off.*

DRE *stops the song.*

So that was... one.

DRE	Only nine hundred and ninety-thousand

They both laugh.

nine hundred and ninety-nine to go.

DES	Pain sells, I guess.
DRE	It does.
DES	But you're not actually saying that *struggle love*
DRE	nah
DES	is, like, healthy – for anyone, right?

DRE	I'm definitely not saying that.
DES	Good.
DRE	I'm *saying* –
DES	Oh?
DRE	...in moderation.
DES	Oh *wow*
DRE	I just mean
DES	I'm *stunned*
DRE	you're making it sound bad
DES	*me?*
DRE	I'm just saying – No one that's ever *loved* someone has lived without struggle.

Beat.

DES	(*Quietly.*) Well maybe we've been through too much to romanticise struggle.
DRE	Sounds like it was lucky timing, then.
DES	I don't know if I believe in luck.
DRE	Why not?
DES	I think we make our own luck.
DRE	But you still met coz of a chain of events you had no control over?
DES	We had control over ourselves.

DRE *laughs.*

What?

He starts playfully but ends intensely:

DRE	When you're *in love* with someone, you can't control it.

	You don't have power over it. It consumes you – all of you and all you can do is just – *be* – in it.
DES	That's not all you can do.
DRE	You think you can control how much you love someone?
DES	Why not?
DRE	(*Smiles*.) That's my line.
DES	I think we can control anything if we try.

She sees his look.

(*Laughs*.) Okay so I *heard* what I said

DRE	there's that Bond villain again
DES	after I *said* what I said
DRE	seek help
DES	I did! Yeeeears of therapy –

They both laugh.

Now I get to call myself a 'recovering perfectionist'.

Beat.

(*Quietly*.) How lucky am I?

DRE	You don't believe in luck, remember.
DES	Touché.

Now she stares at him.

| DRE | (*Holds up his glass*.) You want another? |

She continues to stare.

Des?

Snap.

Two

Past. A university bar.

DES   (*To us.*) You're eighteen. You're in London.
And it's the final night of freshers' week when
it happens.
You see him. Across the room in a bar,
surrounded by a small crowd
like moths to a flame. He looks relaxed
standing there
with his… height, and his face, and his long,
long limbs.
Your eyes follow the curve of his arm till you
see it's attached to –
Oh. A woman. A whole… human woman. You
only see her in profile
but that's enough to know that she's beautiful
and confident
and definitely owns a gym membership.

And now he sees you. And he sees you seeing
her.
And there's a look on his face – a look you
don't recognise –
and then he turns away. Blanks you. Just like
that.
You pretend it doesn't sting.
And remind your legs to keep moving
forward.

(*To* DRE.) Can we talk?

DRE *shrugs casually, but there's an agitated
energy to him.*

Alone?

Another shrug. DES *smiles politely at Human
Woman as she waits for her to leave.*

She seems… nice.

DRE	She is. *Nice*.
DES	(*A curt laugh*.) Okay.
DRE	What?
DES	Nothing.
DRE	What? You don't like it?
DES	What do you think?
DRE	Don't know. How would I know? Not a mind-reader, am I?
DES	Okay, you're mad.
DRE	What d'you want?
DES	This is how it's gonna be, then?
DRE	I got friends waiting.
DES	Friends?
DRE	Yeah. Friends. You know what those are, right?

DES *begins to answer, then stops herself.*

DES	You know what, forget this.

She turns to leave.

DRE	Yeah, just leave then. That's what you do, innit?
DES	Should I stay or should I go, which is it?
DRE	Say what you came here to say. And then cut.
DES	Can we just find somewhere else to –
DRE	Nah. Here's good. Talk.
DES	Fine. (*Takes a breath*.) So, I know you're probably wondering –
DRE	Two months, Des.

Beat.

	You kiss me and then ghost me for two months?
DES	I need you to know –
DRE	Where were you? Why didn't you talk to me? Did I do something wrong?
DES	No. It's not… what you're thinking.
DRE	Okay. So what is it?
DES	It's not –
DRE	not *what*?
DES	that easy.
DRE	It's never easy with you, man!

Long beat.

DES	Right.
DRE	Nah don't make this
DES	I get it
DRE	something *I* did wrong
DES	it's never easy with me, I'm difficult I make everything harder than it needs to be
DRE	don't do that
DES	keep going, I've heard it all before.
DRE	That's not what I'm *saying*
DES	then explain.
DRE	Why? Coz everything's gotta be on your terms?
DES	That's not true.
DRE	Even right now, you're thinking 'man's got a point' but you still want it your way, don't you?

DES	Maybe I can't... just... explain it.
DRE	Why not?
DES	Dre –
DRE	Why *not*?
DES	You're always asking why *not* like it's that *simple*
DRE	coz I'm trying to *understand* you
DES	okay so just *listen*, just listen and let me *think* –
DRE	What's there to think about? You had two months!
DES	I didn't mean to –
DRE	What? Kiss me?
DES	No, that's not
DRE	coz I'm not good enough?
DES	...What?
DRE	That's it, no? Just say it. I didn't grow up like you, I don't live in some fuck-off house with my dad –
DES	What're you *even talking* about right now?
DRE	so if you're not on it
DES	that's not it
DRE	then just *say* you're not on it
DES	just *listen*
DRE	don't ghost me and make me feel like a *dickhead* –
DES	then stop acting like a dickhead!
	Beat.

Can you just – can you *please* just be my
friend right now? Or-or-or pretend?
Can you just pretend that you're my friend
and you're on my side for just like five
seconds –

DRE   that's what I *thought* we were

DES   we were

DRE   you and me, I thought we were real

DES   we are

DRE   friends before anything else

DES   *we are*

DRE   then *why did you leave*?

DES   (*To us.*) You feel him. There.
Scratching beneath the surface
impatient, pushing, *always* pushing

DRE   Come on, man.

DES   (*To us.*) until you have to push back.

DRE   Stop acting like you don't know me.

DES   Well maybe I don't! (*Pauses, then powers
through.*)
And maybe you don't know me.

DRE   So who are you then, Des? Tell me!

DES   (*To us.*) Maybe this is the moment you can
both sense
that something is ending that never truly
began.
Maybe you say something funny or something
clever
that hides how his simple question is
shattering your whole world.
Or maybe you reach for the lie
that has always felt safer than the truth.

She now speaks to him. Her tone is flat,
dismissive.

You're right. Yeah. I'm not on it. Sorry.

DRE *nods slowly. She watches him as he*
walks away.

Going. Going. Gone –

Snap.

Three

DES *stands alone.*

DES   (*To us.*) It's a strange thing. Isn't it?
Living in a Black body and trying to become
aware
of the way your body interacts with the world
and not just the way the world interacts with
your body.

It's almost like unlearning something you
were taught
before you even knew you'd been taught it.
How do you begin to rewire your mind
and train your body to relax into touch –
again?

A body that has been on alert
long before it fully grew into itself.

You're five years old. You're told you look
ten.

You're ten years old. You're told you could be
fifteen.

You're fifteen years old. You're told you're a
grown woman.

You're a grown woman.
And you're wondering why little Black girls
are always treated like they're grown?

You don't have an answer that makes sense.
So you paint.
Bury yourself in a world of colours.
Painting things and places and people and
bodies –
Black bodies and divine bodies and wounded
bodies
and all of the bodies seeking a safe place
where they can rest.

Four

Present. Nana's house.

DES	So where's your... wife?
DRE	We're not married.
DES	Right. Sorry.
DRE	She took Malachi home. He insisted on laying flowers at Nana's grave.
DES	Malachi. You named him after your brother?
	DRE *nods. She smiles.*
	That's nice.
	Pause.
	So you're not married, huh? What's up with that?
DRE	Well, *pastor* –
DES	ha

DRE	we prefer to live in sin, you see.
DES	Oh he's *sassy*, okay.
DRE	What's sexier than eternal damnation? I mean apart from –
BOTH	bus stations.
	They smile.
DES	Yup. That's following me to the grave isn't it?
DRE	'Here lies Destiny. Man did she love bus stations.'
DES	What a legacy.
DRE	What a *life*.
	They laugh. A shift.
	Not everyone wants marriage, Des.
DES	I mean, sure. But *you* do. Or used to. What changed?
DRE	People change. Don't they? (*Lightly.*) Just look at you, innit?
DES	Ohhh. (*Looking at his face.*)
DRE	What?
	(*As she continues to look.*) What is it?
DES	Waaaaait. Did you – propose?
	DRE *doesn't know how to respond.*
	Ohhhh shit. You did, didn't you?
	He shrugs.
	And she...?
DRE	said no.
DES	Ohhhh!
	DES *starts to laugh.*

DRE	Nah, are you seriously –
DES	no, I'm not, I'm not, I'm not laughing –
	She unsuccessfully tries to contain the giggles.
DRE	you're not laughing
DES	(*Laughing.*) no, I'm not
DRE	you're not laughing?
DES	I feel like a detective who just cracked a case
DRE	this is you not laughing, yeah?
DES	(*Covers her mouth.*) help me, I don't know what's happening.
	As DRE *watches her struggle to contain her laughter, he begins to laugh with her.*
DRE	This is messed up, you know
DES	I know
DRE	you're burning in hell for this
DES	then I can save you a seat.
	He laughs. A shift.
DRE	Nah, she was right to say no, though. She – Nina, that's
DES	that's her name?
DRE	Yeah.
DES	*Nina.* Pretty name.
DRE	Yeah.
DES	Is she pretty?
	DRE *laughs awkwardly.*
	What? Is that weird? For me to ask?
DRE	Nah nah

DES   coz you're getting a little

DRE   nah it's calm

DES   a *little* weird

DRE   She's beautiful, yeah.

DES   I bet.

DRE   Damn smart too.

DES   Nice. Remind the people you're not shallow.

                    DRE *laughs again – now much less awkward.*

DRE   Can't lie though, bruised the ego a little.
                    When she first said no.
                    As soon as she said it though, I knew.
                    Like, in my bones. I knew, you know?
                    She was pregnant with Malachi then –
                    and I can't imagine a world where he doesn't
                    exist now
                    but he definitely wasn't planned.
                    Maybe she thought I was just tryin'a reassure
                    her –
                    like it was a knee-jerk reaction, or something,
                    you know?

DES   I can think of worse reactions.

DRE   The more I think about it though, I dunno –
                    I think it was about me. And it wasn't noble or
                    honourable.
                    I spent my whole life – trying to be part of a
                    family.
                    Was *hungry* for it. Know what I mean?
                    And then suddenly life said –
                    'Here you go. Here's your perfect "normal"
                    family. From scratch.'
                    And I just… wanted to protect it. With
                    everything I had.

DES   'Normal family.'

DRE	Right.
DES	What's normal, anyway?
	DRE *looks at her for a beat.*
DRE	Des. Just so you know, Nina and I – it's not – I mean, her and I, we're not –
DES	But you still did it. Though. Right? Created a family. With someone. That you now... *live* with – still?
	Her tone is light, but there's a note of accusation.
	So you got everything you wanted anyway. Right?
DRE	Right.
	***
DES	(*To us.*) You're twenty-seven. You're back. Standing outside the house of the boy who appeared out of nowhere. Except – You see a man. Holding his baby. With someone else.
	Beat.
	Months later, oceans away, you find an article about the myth of first love. It tells you it's down to a chemical system in your brain – an anomaly that fools you into believing it was something profound – instead of just the impact of experiencing something for the first time.
	So each time you feel that tugging in your heart – a reminder of the moment *some* part of you was severed in two –

You pull it out. Read it again. And remember how to breathe.

***

Past.

DES	Do you think we'll get to see it?
DRE	What?
DES	What comes next. After the end of the world?

Snap.

Five

Past. A university bar.

DRE   (*To us*.) It's your twentieth birthday.
You're blowing out candles on a cake
surrounded by people and drinks and music.
And you're wondering how it's possible
for a human being
to feel this lonely –
when it hits you:

You're now older than your older brother.

You feel familiar shadows closing in
as you think about all the people who should
be here
but aren't.

DES *approaches.*

DES   Hi.

DRE   (*To us*.) It's been over a year.

DES   Can I sit?

DRE	(*To us*.) You're wondering if you're hallucinating.
	He slowly brings a hand up – then pokes her face.
DES	Ow.
DRE	(*To us*.) You're not hallucinating.
DES	Are you drunk?
	DRE *nods – for too long.*
	Good. It'll make this easier.
	She smiles at his questioning look.
	Oh. Yeah. I'm kidnapping you.
	***
	Des's uni flat.
DES	(*To us*.) Seemed like a good idea. At the time. But now he's *here*.
	In your flat. And you're trying not to lose your nerve.
DRE	Why am I here?
DES	(*To us*.) He's sobering up.
DRE	Why did you bring me here?
DES	(*To us*.) He's asking logical questions.
	Pause.
	You briefly wonder about Human Woman with the Gym Membership.
DRE	Des?
DES	I wanted… to give you. Something. Um. A gift. Of sorts.
DRE	A gift?

DES	(*To us*.) You pull back a large covering – unveiling something in the centre of the room. And then you wait.

***

He looks at the painting for a long time. Then he looks at her.

DRE	This – is me?

She nods.

(*To us*.) It takes your breath away

DES	You hate it?
DRE	(*To us*.) that someone could look at you
DES	You're not saying anything.
DRE	(*To us*.) and see *this*. All of *this*.
DES	That means you hate it.
DRE	(*To us*.) For the first time in a long time, you feel your muscles relax. Like releasing a breath you never knew you were holding.
DES	Say something.
DRE	Man. It's *beautiful*, Des.
DES	…Yeah?
DRE	Yeah.
DES	(*Smiles*.) Okay. Good. That's good. Now for part two.
DRE	Part two?
DES	I'm going away. Abroad. For this – summer art programme. That I got on because of the painting – because of… you. And it reminded me how you were always… making me brave.

And I've now had – some time, a lot of time, to think.
And I think that you. Are important. To me.
So I don't wanna lose you from my life.

DRE   What are you –

DES   Just hear me out. Let me get this out.

DRE   You don't have to.

DES   I want to, now. I do.

Beat.

DRE   Okay.

***

DES   (*To us.*) And so you tell him. You tell him everything.
Everything that happened.
Everything that was packaged away
and left to rot in plain sight.

You tell him about The Girl Who Floated Away
when something was taken from her –
when a trusted family friend
made her believe her body was no longer her own
and all she remembered was the smell of cinnamon.

You tell him about the panic attacks that started.
You tell him about her papa.
Who stopped talking.
Who didn't have the words to mend her heart – or his own
and in the absence of words they created a new language
with academic achievements.

You tell him about her mama – and wonder
who she would've been
if they only had more time.

And when there's nothing left to tell –
you stop. And you wait. And you wait.
And you wait.

A very long silence.

DRE   I'm here.

Beat.

I'm here.

Beat.

I'm here.

DES   (*To us*.) It starts in your soul. Makes its way
into your mind.
And then finally, you feel it – sitting there – in
your body.
It wraps itself around your heart
filling it with light
and then gently
quietly

explodes it.

Beat.

It's a powerful thing to be seen.

END OF PART THREE

IV. LOVERS

One

They stare at each other. Carefully, tentatively take each other in. Then finally, DES *smiles.*

DES   Hi.

Beat.

DRE   Hi.

***

Past.

DES   (*To us.*) There's an energy between you
when you get back from overseas –
when you become friends again –
but not friends. No.
Something else...
something undefined
something still taking shape –
caught in the act of metamorphosis.
Something is shifting between you – again.
Something terrifying – and comforting.
You both dance around it
– while no one makes a move.

'Situationship' by Snoh Aalegra plays.

So are you still with... (*Painfully tries for subtlety.*) Gym... Membership?

DRE   ...Huh?

DES   (*Quickly.*) Never mind.

DRE   (*Looking at his body in alarm.*) Do I still go gym?

DES	(*Mumbles, walking away.*) Not what I'm asking.
DRE	(*Following.*) Why are you saying it like that? Where you goin'?
DES	I DON'T KNOW!
	Snap.

Two

Present. Nana's house. They've been drinking for a while.

DRE	Seriously, where you goin' though?
DES	To get more
DRE	*more* booze? What happened to helping me pack up?
DES	This is the good stuff, okay! Don't get all stingy now.
DRE	How drunk are you?
DES	(*Firmly.*) No.
DRE	…That wasn't a yes or no question.
DES	Yes.
DRE	You're still getting on that plane later though. Right?
	Beat. The question sobers her up a little.
DES	Right.
	Beat.
DRE	So listen to this. My son's first day of school comes round, right.

And it's a big change, you know? But the little
man does his best.
We come home, have dinner, go to bed.
Next morning, I get him up – and d'you know
what he says to me?

DES   What?

DRE   'I already went yesterday.'

        They both laugh.

DES   Naaaah wait 'I already went yesterday.'

        She laughs harder.

DRE   I'm telling you – it took me *out*.

DES   That kid is speaking to my *soul*.

DRE   Straight up.

DES   How do you even argue with that?

DRE   I couldn't!

        They laugh.

        A shift.

        I think about the world when we were
        growing up.
        Like how I had Nana. And even if the world
        was on fire –
        the world was still better with her in it. I was
        better.
        Malachi's not gonna have that, now. You
        know?
        All he's gonna have is –

DES   you.

DRE   Yeah.

DES   And Nina.

DRE   Yeah.

I don't know if I'm –
if, on my own –
if I could ever be... you know

DES   You are.

DRE   I don't know, man.

He looks away, uncertain.

I really don't know.

She looks at him with intention.

DES   (*Firmly.*) You're enough, Dre. I promise.

Snap.

Three

Past. A dark bedroom. DRE *sits alone.*

We hear the muted sound of pumping music on the other side of the door.

DRE   (*To us.*) You're twenty-one. It's Graduation
Night.
And you're alone in some bedroom at some
party in some house.
Thinking back to earlier in the day – when
you got your diploma.
When you looked out into the crowd, saw the
tears in your nana's eyes.
The joy she didn't even try to contain – as she
jumped up from her seat,
and she whooped and she yelled and she told
everyone 'that's my blood'.

He nods.

'That's my blood.'

And it's enough –
should be enough
would've been enough
if your eyes didn't travel to the empty chair on
her left.
The empty chair where the woman who gave
birth to you
should be. Could be. Said she'd be.
But isn't.

You waited five years just to hear her proudly
say those words:
'That's my blood.'
But instead, there's just an empty chair
– and a text saying 'sorry'.

It's almost funny.
Five years of keeping it together –
keeping it easy, keeping it moving
and moving and *always* moving –
and an empty chair is your undoing.
Coz that's what you are –
Undone.
You know it.
You're spiralling and you can't stop it.
Familiar shadows are closing in
the air's running out
the room's growing darker
and darker and darker and –

*Suddenly a bright light filters through, and the
muted music becomes louder.*

DES *enters the room.*

*We hear a snippet of a song that would've
been playing eleven years ago.*

*Perhaps it's something like 'Take Care' by
Drake feat. Rihanna.*

DES   Jeeeez, there you are!

DRE *looks away as she approaches*.

Why's it so dark in here?

A glance around the room.

…'cha doing, weirdo?
You're being summoned for pics with drunk
fools downstairs. Come.

DRE	I'll catch you up in a sec.
DES	Yeah right, like I'm heading back on my own? D'you know how annoying those clowns are when you're sober?

She waits for a response.

And *why* am I still sober, I hear you ask? Well
Dre – turns out,
looking for someone all night diminishes your
ability to get lit.
Who knew?

Pause.

What? No snarky response?

DRE	She didn't come.
DES	'She'? What, you've got a nickname for your brand of sarcasm now?

Silence.

Dre?

DRE	I guess Lagos to London's a long trip, innit. Dunno why I thought she'd make it.
DES	(*Gently.*) …Your mum?

He shrugs.

DRE	Still thought she might. Graduation and all.
DES	Oh Dre, I'm sorry she wasn't there.

DRE	I'm cool.
	She looks at him. Facing away from her. The opposite of cool.
DES	Yeah yeah you seem cool.
DRE	I'm cool.
DES	I know you are.
DRE	So why are you looking at me like that?
DES	How d'you know how I'm looking at you when you haven't looked at me once?
	He still doesn't look at her.
DRE	I don't think I even blame her, you know?
DES	What do you mean?
DRE	I'd do the same.
DES	This isn't your fault
DRE	makes sense actually
DES	Dre
DRE	when you think about it
DES	listen to me
DRE	No!

He finally faces her – unravelling.

Coz what would *you* do? Huh?
If *you* left your home and everyone you loved
for some foreign land?
If *you* crossed oceans for a man that never
knew peace?
If *you* got left behind with two young kids coz
he offed himself?

DES *is reacting to this information for the
first time.*

DES   …Dre –

DRE   And the kid you loved the most –
               well, if he's dead now too and you're just left
               with *me* –
               yeah, makes sense, don't it? That I wouldn't
               be enough?
               It makes sense. You'd do the same, wouldn't
               you?

               She takes a step towards him. He takes a step
               back.

               Throw me away? Make me someone else's
               problem?
               Pack your bags, go back, start a new life with
               a new family?
               It just makes sense, don't it? That she didn't
               choose me?
               Coz why would she?

               Beat.

               Why didn't she?

               Beat.

               Why didn't she… choose *me*?

               He looks away. Angry, embarrassed, hurt.

               The song transforms into a slower
               arrangement.

               DES *looks at him intently – then takes a*
               steadying breath.

DES   I would.

               And as she steps towards him, the scene now
               begins to feel transcendent.

               And I do.

               She lays a hand on his back. Gently holds his
               arm. They stay here for a moment.

Until he finally turns around and allows her to hold him in her embrace.

Something is shifting. After a moment, she gently pulls him towards the centre of the room.

And she leans forward with intention.

DRE   Wait, Des –

He gives her a long, searching look, that seems to be asking:

'Are you sure?'

DES *nods.*

When DRE *doesn't move, she closes the gap between them.*

DES   I'm choosing this.

Beat.

I'm choosing *you.*

DES *lays a hand on* DRE's *cheek.*

Beat.

They kiss.

Beat.

The kiss deepens.

Beat.

They make love.

***

DES   (*To us.*) Before you know it, you're painting
two infinite beings.
Bodies entangled, cosmic, divine
like there's no beginning or end –
only shapes that shift for eternity
from this life and into the next.

You call it 'The Fugitives'.

Based on the memory of lives lived
and not yet lived.

Snap.

Four

Present. Nana's house.

The whiskey bottle is nearly empty. And we can tell.

*Different items from unpacked boxes have spilled out next to
them.*

DES	It's like... like you know when you're home alone, yeah? And you hear a strange noise? Like, any noise? And your brain goes, 'Yup! This is it, man! This is how you die'? *She waits, then, before he can speak:* No, of course not, you're a man.
DRE	That's not fair
DES	(*Laughs.*) then I don't wanna be fair, any more! Man, I used to be *so* jealous of you.
DRE	Of me? Swear?
DES	Yeah! Still am. You just have this *way*. Of being. Of making people *feel* around you. And in New York I didn't – have that, you know? Like... even with my work getting noticed, when it seemed like I could *do* anything and *be* anything – still just... felt like I was *waiting*.

DRE	Waiting for what?
DES	Something bad to happen? Or, I dunno. Something worse – than the last thing? And now I don't even know how to just *feel* good things when they're happening, you know? Like, I'm just thinking about when they'll end? I mean, I'm with a *good* man, who loves me, who *wants* me, who wants my *children*, and I can't even...
	She stops, embarrassed.
	Sorry, I'm chatting shit, no one wants to hear all this!
DRE	I do.
DES	(*Standing up suddenly.*) Don't listen to me, I'm drunk!
DRE	Wanna listen to you even more, now.
	She riffles through a nearby box. Finds a small jewellery box.
DES	Oh! Dre, look!
	She opens it, gasps, showing it to him.
DRE	That's Nana's ring.
DES	It's so beautiful.
DRE	She wanted to be buried with her wedding ring. And left this one for me.
DES	Oh my God. I have a great idea. (*Giggles.*) Dre?
DRE	(*Suspiciously.*) What?
	She gets down on one knee. Holds out the ring.

DES	Will you marry me?
	DRE *stares at her.*
	Get it? Coz of earlier? When I laughed? Now you get to say –
DRE	Yes.
DES	(*Laughs.*) No, you're supposed to get me back by saying –
DRE	(*Firmly.*) Yes.
	She stops laughing.
	Now what?
	Long beat.
	Snap.

Five

Past. Des's flatshare.

DES	What d'you mean 'now what?' Did you use my conditioner?
DRE	Huh?
DES	You heard me.
DRE	Which one's yours?
DES	Dre, man! I leave you in my flat for *one hour* –
DRE	I got confused
DES	oh, *confused*
DRE	just grabbed whatever

DES	grabbed *whatever*
DRE	whatever was there already
DES	It wasn't there.
DRE	Huh?
DES	It was in the cupboard. Under the sink. Away from the shower.
DRE	…Whaaaat?
DES	Dre –
DRE	Okay I'm sorry! It just smells so nice!
DES	You couldn't just use that Shea Moisture one?
DRE	After they switched up the formula? Nah, man!
DES	(*Trying not to laugh.*) How'd you even know that?
DRE	I listen innit
DES	selective
DRE	when you talk
DES	sometimes
DRE	most times
DES	except the times when I tell you to not use my expensive conditioner.
DRE	I'll buy you more.
DES	That's not the point. Why d'you use so much?
DRE	Aren't you supposed to?
DES	This stuff's hella concentrated. You're supposed to add water.
DRE	Like squash?

DES *now laughs, giving up on being annoyed.*

DES	Yeah, I guess.
DRE	Was wondering why I got mad tangles.
DES	You're supposed to work it through.
DRE	I got tired. Seen all these knots?
	When she touches his head, he leans into her touch, nestling.
	I flew too close to the sun.
DES	Okay, Icarus. Come. Let's fix this mess you made.
	She sits him down, and starts to untangle his knots.
DRE	Ow!
DES	Sorry!
	After a few moments:
DRE	Owww, man!
DES	Sorry, did that hurt?
DRE	Yes!
	DES *quickly kisses his forehead apologetically.*
	DRE *smiles blissfully, immediately content.*
	A few moments later, he makes another pained noise.
	(*Pointing to his cheek.*) Owww.
	She rolls her eyes, but pecks him on the cheek.
	(*Points to his other cheek.*) And here.
	DES *complies.*
	(*Points to his lips.*) And here, too.
	She laughs, and pecks him on the mouth.

Actually, *everywhere* is –

She drowns out his next request by tickling him as they both laugh.

***

They stare at each other. Carefully, tentatively take each other in. Then finally, DES *smiles.*

DES   Hi.

Beat.

DRE   Hi.

And as the scene begins to transform:

You think you're funny, don't you?

Snap.

Six

Present. Nana's house.

DES *is holding a bouquet of flowers and pretending to walk down the aisle.*

DES   You're the one who said yes. The game is the
               game, playa.

               *She picks up nearest random object, hands it
               to* DRE.

               Go on, Mister Vicar's not got all day.

DRE   Mister Vicar

DES   yup

DRE   that's his... name?

DES   look, I don't make the rules, man

DRE	think you *might* make up *some* rules
DES	hush now, sweetness, it's our wedding day! And we must now say our vows. Unless – of course, you didn't write yours?
DRE	Oh it's like that?
DES	If you didn't wanna prioritise *me* in the same way
DRE	naaah, I got my vows.
DES	Really?

DRE sets aside whatever object DES handed him. Gently taps his chest.

DRE	Got 'em right here.
DES	Oh, you do?
DRE	(*Nods.*) You ready?
DES	Are you?
DRE	Yes I am.
DES	Take it away!
DRE	I, Dre
DES	yes
DRE	take you, Destiny
DES	that's me
DRE	to be my partner in crime
DES	uh-huh
DRE	forever.
DES	(*Laughing.*) Okay. Not bad.

Pause.

That's it, though?

He looks at her.

DRE   I can say more.

Taking a leaf from her book, DRE *now turns to the imagined crowd – and suddenly we, the audience, become a part of their wedding ceremony.*

You see, friends, family

(*Turns to the imaginary vicar.*) Mister Vicar

DES   crowd work, nice

DRE   I… buried my nana today.

Beat.

I was sent to live with this amazing woman – when I was sixteen
in this small town that she loved so much
and I think – I think it probably saved my life.

When you're young, you know, you take the connections you build for granted.
You think maybe… I don't know, you think you'll have them again –
but that doesn't always happen. Does it?
Sometimes it's just… lightning in a bottle.
Sometimes it's just once – in a lifetime.

He looks back at her.

You think you'll get another shot. But by the time you're ready, you know,
by the time you're – you're coming back up for air, life has other plans.
Takes you to places – places you never expected. But eventually –

DES   Dre, maybe we shouldn't –

DRE   *eventually* – you end up exactly where you're supposed to be.

He now speaks with complete clarity.

And here. In this moment. Is exactly where
I'm supposed to be.

Because here is where I pledge my life to you,
Des.

He takes her hand.

I'm not sure what I believe about other lives
or other worlds, or other dimensions...
But what I *feel*, deep in my bones
is that if soulmates are real –
then Des you have always been mine.
You always believed in me.
And I believe in you.
And when you believe in someone,
it's not just for a moment
or for a while.
It's forever.

A long beat.

DES *doesn't know what to do. They stare at
each other.*

*And it feels like this could be the moment. The
moment they both finally give in.*

Just as DES *is about to close the gap –*

the sudden, loud ringing sound of DRE*'s
phone cuts through the silence.*

DES   (*Without breaking eye contact.*) You should
        probably get that.

DRE   I don't – think so.

        The phone continues to ring. DRE *continues
        to ignore it.*

        Finally, DES *looks away to dig the phone out
        of his pocket.*

        *And freezes. She shakes her head, as if waking
        from a dream.*

She drops DRE's *hand. The magic is gone.*
She hands him the phone.

DES   Take it. It's your family.

He reaches a hand out towards her and –

Snap.

END OF PART FOUR

V. FUGITIVES

One

Past. A flat.

DES	No notes! You nailed that.
	She laughs as he spins her around.
	My mama would be very impressed with your *ngai-ngai*.
DRE	D'you think?
DES	I do. Tell me the dream again. After business school.
	He says it with the flourish of a man who's repeated it many times.
DRE	Okay! West and Central African cuisine.
DES	Yes
DRE	My nana's food
DES	okay
DRE	meets your mama's food
DES	uh-huh
DRE	in a perfect fusion
DES	that's right!
	***
DRE	So it's *my* fault?
DES	Yes, you don't teach me enough Yoruba! And I've taught you bare phrases in Lingala. Come on. Say something to me in Yoruba.
	Beat.

DRE	Mo nifẹ rẹ.
DES	What does that mean?

He looks at her. And just smiles.

***

DES *is dancing to 'No One Like You' by P-Square (or the same classic Afrobeat song played in the earlier scene).* DRE *watches in amusement.*

***

DES	Do you think we'll get to see it?
DRE	What?
DES	What comes next. After the end of the world?
DRE	Maybe we already have.

***

DRE	A year's residency?
DES	In Prague. What do you think?
DRE	...I think it's great, Des.
DES	Yeah?
DRE	Yeah! What's a year anyway, right?

***

DRE *is dancing to 'Karolina' by Awilo Longomba or 'Loi' by Koffi Olomide (or the same classic Congolese rumba song played in the earlier scene).* DES *watches in amusement.*

***

DES	My painting. I can't – find it?
DRE	What d'you mean?

DES	For my portfolio. 'The Fugitives'. How does a painting just *disappear*?
DRE	You named a painting... 'The Fugitives'? And it's just gone and... escaped?
	***
DRE	(*In frustration.*) Fuck!
DES	You're not your dad.
DRE	You don't know what it's like. In my head, sometimes
DES	you're *not* your dad
DRE	you *don't know* –
DES	so *talk* to me! Okay? Just... just keep talking.
	***
DRE	Sorry I missed it.
DES	Where were you? Been trying you all day.
DRE	Phone's been off, sorry.
	Pause.
DES	...You're okay. Though. Right?
	***
DRE	Two years? In New York?
DES	We don't have to decide now. I don't even have to take it.
DRE	Why wouldn't you take it?
DES	You don't – think I'd have a reason – to stay? Here?
DRE	Do you... have a reason to stay?
	***
DRE	(*To us.*) You feel familiar shadows closing in.

DES	(*To us.*) You feel him changing shape. Getting blurry.
DRE	(*To us.*) This time, you let them.

***

DES	Talk to me!

***

DES	(*To us.*) The next fairy tale you illustrate you call 'The Boy Who Lost His Smile.'

***

DES	So, you think I *should?* Take it... then?
DRE	...Yeah. Why not?

He turns away from her. She waits.

DES	So that's it then?

Silence.

***

DES   (*To us.*) Before you leave for New York, you go home.

And when you open the door, you hear your Mama's song.

Yolele' by Papa Wemba plays, as if from far away.

It makes you cry. And you can't stop. And then your papa appears.
He looks older than you remember. When you were last paying attention.
You feel her. Mama. Here. Wrapping you both in her embrace.
Papa doesn't say anything for a long time.
And when he speaks, he says:
'I am sorry you only had me. When she was the one you deserved.'

It's the first time you realise you were all he
had left too.

***

DRE   (*To us*.) You're twenty-four.
You return to your nana's town to care for her
failing health.
It'll be years before you realise that she was
the one caring for yours.

And it will be years after this
weeks before she takes her final breath and
becomes an ancestor,
that she will turn to you and say:
'The only thing that makes this easier
is knowing I am leaving this world before
you.
Thank you for giving me that. Now hold on.
You understand?
I will not see you before it is time.
So hold on – and keep holding on
my son.'

And so you do.

Two

Present. Crossroads.

DRE   Cab's on its way.

            DES *nods.* DRE *takes something out of a box.*
            He hands it to her.

DES   …What's this?

DRE   It's yours.

            As she turns, we see it's a painting.

DES	'The Fugitives'? My painting. It was… here… all along?
DRE	Yeah.
DES	How did it –
DRE	I took it.
	She looks at him, for a long beat. Then back at the painting again.
DES	…You took it?
	Something is clearly stirring inside her. She becomes agitated. Fidgety.
	You said the cab is –
DRE	On its way. Yeah.
	Pause.
	Can I ask you something? Before you go?
DES	(*Apprehensively.*) What?
DRE	Are you happy?
	Beat.
DES	…don't do that
DRE	What?
DES	that *thing* people do
DRE	I mean with your life? Travis?
DES	when they think they know –
DRE	You said you just got engaged
DES	been engaged for a year, actually.
DRE	A year?
DES	Yeah.
DRE	And you didn't tell anyone?

DES	Who's 'anyone'?
	Beat.
DRE	When's the wedding?
DES	I don't know.
DRE	You don't know?
DES	We don't have a date yet.
DRE	You don't have a date?
DES	*Yet.*
DRE	*Yet.* Why not?
DES	I don't know, Dre. Wanna be our wedding planner?
DRE	I wanna know if you're happy?
DES	Of course I'm happy.
DRE	Are you?
DES	Yes!
DRE	Okay.
	Beat.
DES	What's that supposed to mean?
DRE	Okay, you're happy.
DES	That's what I said.
DRE	That's good.
DES	It is.
DRE	That's great.
DES	*I* think so.
DRE	Sensational.
	Beat.

DES	What're you doing?
DRE	I'm not doing anything
DES	(*Imitating*.) 'Sensational.' When have you ever said 'sensational'
DRE	(*Feigning lightness*.) you don't know my life
DES	but you think you know mine? What do you want me to *say*, Dre? That I'm miserable?
DRE	Are you?

She just looks at him.

Des?

DES	I need to get away from you.
DRE	Des –
DES	This! See this? This is why I didn't –

She stops herself.

DRE	Didn't what?
DES	*You.* You make me –
DRE	make you what? You can talk to me.

He reaches out a hand –

DES	Don't *touch* me!

Beat.

Sorry. I didn't – mean to be that dramatic.

But seriously don't *touch* me, you are – driving me insane. Okay?
Making me question things that don't matter.

DRE	Like what?
DES	Like I don't know, Dre. Useless, stupid, nonsensical things

DRE	okay good
DES	like if there was even a fraction of truth in this idea of – of of 'soulmates' or whatever the hell you wanted to call it, then how do we only get... one? I mean, come on! If every decision you made led you to where you are now – that means there are paths you didn't choose, right? So if you chose a different path, you'd probably have a different life, in a different world, with a different person, right? So that means there *has* to be more than one out there for us. Because if the idea is that this, this, this, I don't even know, this *soul connection* you have with just *one person* can never be replicated or matched by *anyone else* – (*Rising anger.*) what do you even do with that? No, no, *fuck that* – and you know what, *fuck you*
DRE	oi –
DES	for making me feel like I took *everything* I could ever feel for a person and put it all into you.
	Beat.
	Do you know how *insane* that is? It is, right? It's insane. It's an insane thing that normal people do *not* do
DRE	what's normal, anyway?
DES	*normal* is not sabotaging every relationship you ever had for an *idea*. Okay?
	Beat.
	It's not wondering what could've been and always thinking maybe it could've been better. And it's not rationalising these feelings for something that never – really – *was*.

DRE   You didn't stay!

DES   You didn't ask!

               Beat.

               (*Quietly.*) You didn't ask.

               Beat.

DRE   I'm asking now.

               Beat.

               Stay.

               Long beat.

DES   I think. When it didn't – when *we* didn't –
               work – when I failed –
               I think I buried all of that *feeling* somewhere
               no one else could find.
               And then I lost... the key? Or something.
               That's what it feels like.
               Like I lost the key, and now I'm stuck here,
               feeling numb
               like there's a part of me that's missing
               and I don't know how to make my way back
               or how to move forward. So I'm just stuck, at
               this crossroads
               looking at all these paths in front of me, and
               I can't – move.

DRE   You didn't fail.

DES   I couldn't... help you, Dre! The way you
               helped me. So yeah. I failed.

DRE   ...Is that what you think?
               Des? How can you not know that you changed
               my whole life?

               (*Seeing her shake her head.*) You did.

               (*Seeing her look away.*) Des. You did.

DRE *stares at her for a long beat – and in this moment, something starts shifting for him.*

When he next speaks, he's deceptively casual.

You know, you taught me something. A long time ago.
Taught me to wait. Be still.
Listen to what's happening in the silence.
I never forgot that.

Beat.

So.

Loudly and suddenly claps his hands together.

Quick-fire. For… you and me. Go.

She looks at him like homie just lost his whole damn mind.

DES	…What are you doing?
DRE	Go!
DES	I'm not in the mood for –
DRE	Trust me. Please?

Beat. Then, reluctantly:

DES	Why would I argue for you and me?
DRE	Someone once told me you should know your opponent's argument.
DES	(*Flatly.*) There's no argument.
DRE	Prove it.

She shakes her head.

DES	…This is… stupid.
DRE	I'm too – short.
DES	What?
DRE	Too – ugly.
DES	Where?

DRE	I have dimples.
DES	So?
DRE	Dimples suck.
DES	Oh my God *shut up*.
DRE	I don't come from money.
DES	Why would I care about that?
DRE	I have a kid.
DES	There's no reality where something made from *you*... could be a bad thing.

They share a tender look.

DRE	I let you go. When I couldn't –
DES	That wasn't your fault.
DRE	Then tell me –

Beat.

Why do you still think it was yours?

This is it. The single thing she doesn't have an answer for.

After a moment, he forces himself to continue.

This isn't where you need to be. Any more. Is it?

Beat.

You made a life somewhere else. With someone else.

Beat.

With a man that loves you.

Beat.

And you – love him – too?

Long beat. This is an emotional moment for DES, who might have never said this before.

DES   Yeah.

                       DRE *nods. It's a blow he's been preparing to*
                       take, but he feels it all the same.

                       After a moment, he puts on a playful smile and
                       powers through.

DRE   And even though I really just wanna say:
                       'fuck that guy and fuck his lil jazz band too'

                       DES *lets out a short unexpected laugh.*

                       there isn't a universe where I tell you you
                       don't deserve this.
                       Coz you do, Des. Deserve love.
                       Big, epic, hell, even *easy* love – (*A smile.*) –
                       why not?
                       However you want it, you deserve it all.

                       DES *is overwhelmed. Like something, inside*
                       her, is being set free.

                       So stop being afraid. Stop trying to *control* it.
                       Let it in. *Feel* it. Feel it all.

                       And so she does.

                       And maybe the opening chords of Alice
                       Smith's majestic cover of 'I Put a Spell on You'
                       return.
                       And maybe the space begins to shift, and shift,
                       and shift.
                       And maybe we see – hear – feel – all of these
                       moments as they coalesce.

                       As they interrupt the space, colliding and
                       transforming and shifting in and out of each
                       other as they are remembered, and honoured,
                       and released.

                       They are mostly inaudible – echoes, hints,
                       ghosts that we don't quite catch. But we feel
                       them.

DES	*Then what was it about?*
DRE	*What do you think, Des?*
DES	*So I'm just saying. That you can stop.* *Sometimes.*
DRE	*So who are you then, Des? Tell me.*
DES	*Talk to me!*
DRE	*Why didn't she choose me?*
DES	*I do.*
DRE	*I'm here.*
DES	*I'm choosing this.*
DRE	*Mo nife rẹ.*
DES	*I'm choosing you.*

As this is happening, DES gives DRE 'The Fugitives' painting back.
She's leaving it behind. He hesitates.
And then, finally, he takes it. Their hands connect and linger on the painting.
Whatever feels right for the actors to do at this moment – they do just that.

Then DES leaves.

And finally, DRE places the painting back in the box it came from.

We can only just about make out this final moment:

DES	*Do you think we'll get to see it?*
DRE	*What?*
DES	*What comes next. After the end of the world?*
DRE	*Maybe we already have.*
DES	*Oh yeah? And what did it look like?*

DRE   *Two little Black kids*
                       destined to form each other –
                       again and again.

                       Snap.

Three

DRE *stands alone, on a decluttered stage that looks exactly as it
did in the beginning.*

The complete silence rings loudly.

We sit in it.

For the longest beat.

Until –

***

DES *enters, slightly out of breath.*

*They stare at each other. Carefully, tentatively take each other
in. Then finally,* DES *smiles.*

DES   Hi.

                       *Maybe we are witnessing a past moment we
                       have already seen before*

                       or a present moment that changes everything

                       *or another moment that exists somewhere
                       beyond the periphery.*

                       We don't hear what comes next.

                       And maybe this is where we end.

END

Bush Theatre

We make theatre for London. Now.

For over 50 years the Bush Theatre has been a world-famous home for new plays and an internationally renowned champion of playwrights.

Combining ambitious artistic programming with meaningful community engagement work and industry leading talent development schemes, the Bush Theatre champions and supports unheard voices to develop the artists and audiences of the future.

Since opening in 1972 the Bush has produced more than 500 ground-breaking premieres of new plays, developing an enviable reputation for its acclaimed productions nationally and internationally.

They have nurtured the careers of writers including James Graham, Lucy Kirkwood, Temi Wilkey, Jonathan Harvey and Jack Thorne. Recent successes include Tyrell Williams' *Red Pitch*, Benedict Lombe's *Shifters*, and Arinzé Kene's *Misty*. The Bush has won over 100 awards including the Olivier Award for Outstanding Achievement in Affliate Theatre for the past four years for Richard Gadd's *Baby Reindeer*, Igor Memic's *Old Bridge*, Waleed Akhtar's *The P Word* and Matilda Feyiṣayọ Ibini's *Sleepova*.

Located in the renovated old library on Uxbridge Road in the heart of Shepherd's Bush, the Bush Theatre continues to create a space where all communities can be part of its future and call the theatre home.

'The place to go for ground-breaking work as diverse as its audiences' EVENING STANDARD

bushtheatre.co.uk
@bushtheatre